THE ROMANTIC
COMPOSERS

—

ROBERT SCHUMANN

From a water color made in Vienna in his youth

The ROMANTIC COMPOSERS

===

BY

DANIEL GREGORY MASON

AUTHOR OF "FROM GRIEG TO BRAHMS,"
"BEETHOVEN AND HIS FORERUNNERS," ETC.

——

"Consciously or unconsciously a new school is being
founded on the basis of the Beethoven-Schubert romanticism, a school which we may venture to expect will mark
a special epoch in the history of art."   SCHUMANN

——

AMS PRESS
NEW YORK

105755

Reprinted from the edition of 1906, New York
First AMS EDITION published 1970
Manufactured in the United States of America

International Standard Book Number: 404-04223-6

Library of Congress Card Catalog Number: 73-119654

AMS PRESS, INC.
NEW YORK, N.Y. 10003

PREFACE

THIS book completes the series of studies of composers and of their music, from Palestrina to the present day, which was begun with "From Grieg to Brahms" (1902), and continued in "Beethoven and his Forerunners" (1904). It will be noted that these three volumes should be read in an order different from that of their publication. First should come "Beethoven and his Forerunners," in which are made a general survey of the periods of musical history and the principles of musical style, and special studies of Palestrina, Bach, Haydn, Mozart, and Beethoven; then "The Romantic Composers," in which the story is taken up at the death of Beethoven and carried through the period of romanticism, with essays on Schubert, Schumann, Mendelssohn,

Chopin, Berlioz, and Liszt; and finally "From Grieg to Brahms," comprising studies of the chief modern musicians, including Grieg, Dvořák, Saint-Saëns, Franck, Tschaïkowsky, and Brahms, and two more general papers on "The Appreciation of Music" and "The Meaning of Music." Thus read, the three books should serve as a commentary on the more important individual composers, æsthetic principles, and historical schools in modern instrumental music.

From the first I have had in mind the intention of illuminating the musical peculiarities of each composer by constant reference to his personal character and temperament. For this reason, while I have dealt as briefly as possible with colorless biographical facts, I have made free use of characteristic anecdotes, of contemporary descriptions of appearance, manners, etc., and of letters and table-talk where they are available. Music is indeed a unique artistic medium, and no man can express anything in it except through a technical mastery which has little to do with his character. Yet, given the medium, what he does express is bound to be permeated with his peculiar personality; and as the general reader can get a much clearer idea of a human being like himself than he can of so subtle a technique as that of music, it has seemed better to lay stress on that side, even though it is not the only or perhaps even the most important one. With the object of keeping awake, nevertheless, the reader's sense of those technical methods and traditions which so largely determine the nature of all music, I have included in each book some pages dealing with impersonal principles and historical schools.

Believing that one has no right to intrude, in such studies as these, one's own prejudices, but should transcend as far as possible one's temperamental limitations, I had hoped to be able to maintain throughout the attitude of the chronicler, and to exclude all special pleading. In the essays on Berlioz and Liszt I have perhaps not achieved this detachment of attitude. Realism is a tendency which seems to me quite mistaken and mischievous in music, and I have attacked it with some warmth. But in view of the great favor that realism enjoys in contemporary composition, the shoals of writers that rally every day to its defence, and the potency of its appeal to the average listener, whose dramatic sense and pictorial imagination are always livelier than his purely musical perception, I do not greatly fear that I shall dangerously disturb any reader's critical equilibrium.

These studies are intended simply as guides to the music they discuss. If they lead the reader to the concert-hall, to the piano, to the library of scores; if they help him to hear themes and their development where before he heard only masses of agreeable sound; if they incite him to repeat and analyze his musical experiences, to listen with his mind as well as his ears, to study a symphony as alertly as he would study a painting or an essay, — then only will they have justified their existence.

WASHINGTON, CONNECTICUT,
October 17, 1906.

CONTENTS

—

LIST OF ILLUSTRATIONS

—

I
INTRODUCTION
ROMANTICISM IN MUSIC
—

I

INTRODUCTION
ROMANTICISM IN MUSIC

—

*

I

HISTORIANS of music are accustomed to speak of the first half or three-quarters of the nineteenth century as the Romantic Period in music, and of those composers who immediately follow Beethoven, including Schubert, Schumann, Mendelssohn, Berlioz, Chopin, Liszt, and some others, as the Romantic Composers. The word "romantic," as thus used, forms no doubt a convenient label; but if we attempt to explain its meaning, we find ourselves involved in several difficulties. Were there then no romanticists before Schubert? Have no composers written romantically since 1870? Such questions, arising at once, lead us inevitably to the more general inquiry, What *is* romanticism?

In the broadest sense in which the word "romanticism" can be used, the sense in which it is taken, for example, by Pater in the Postscript of his "Appreciations," it seems to mean simply interest in novel and strange elements of artistic effect. "It is the addition of strangeness to beauty," says Pater, "that constitutes the romantic character in art; and the desire of beauty being a fixed element in every artistic organization, it is the addition of curiosity to this desire of beauty that constitutes the romantic temper." Romanticism is thus the innovating spirit, as opposed to the conserving spirit of classicism; romanticists appear in every age and school; and Stendhal is right in saying that "all good art was romantic in its day." It is interesting, in passing, to note the relation of this definition to the widely prevalent notion that romanticism is extravagant and lawless. To the mind wedded to tradition all novelty is extravagant; and since an artistic form is grasped only after considerable practice, all new forms necessarily appear formless at first. Hence, if we begin by saying that romantic art is novel and strange art, it requires only a little inertia or intolerance in our point of view to make us add that it is grotesque and irrational art, or in fact not art at all. Critics have often been known to arrive at this conclusion.

Suggestive as Pater's definition is, however, it is obviously too vague and sweeping to carry us far in our quest. It does not explain why Monteverde, with his revolutionary dominant seventh chords, or the Florentine composers of the early seventeenth century, with their unheard-of free recitative, were not quite as genuine romanticists as Schubert with his whimsical modulation and Schumann with his harsh dissonances. We have still to ask why, instead of appending our label of "romantic" to the innovators of centuries earlier than the nineteenth, we confine it to that comparatively small group of men who immediately followed Beethoven.

The answer is to be found in the distinctness of the break that occurred in musical development at this time, the striking difference in type between the compositions of Beethoven and those of his successors. From Philipp Emanuel

Bach up to Beethoven, the romanticism of each individual composer merely carried him a step forward on a well-established path; it prompted him to refine here, to pare away there, to expand this feature, to suppress that, in a scheme of art constantly maturing, but retaining always its essential character. With Beethoven, however, this particular scheme of art, of which the type is the sonata, with its high measure of formal beauty and its generalized expression, reached a degree of perfection beyond which it could not for the moment go. The romantic impulse toward novelty of Beethoven's successors had to satisfy itself, therefore, in some other way than by heightening abstract æsthetic beauty or general expressiveness; until new technical resources could be developed the limit was reached in those directions. Beethoven had himself, meanwhile, opened the door on an inviting vista of possibilities in a new field — that of highly specialized, idiosyncratic, subjective expression. He had shown how music, with Mozart so serene, detached, and impersonal, could become a language of personal feeling, of individual passion, even of whim, fantasy, and humor. It was inevitable that those who came after him should seek their novelty, should satisfy their curiosity, along this new path of subjectivism and specialized expression. And as this music of the person, as we may call it, which now began to be written, was different not only in degree but in kind from the objective art which prepared the way for it, it is natural that in looking back upon so striking a new departure we should give it a special name, such as romanticism.

As for the other line of demarcation, which separates the romantic period from what we call the modern, that is purely arbitrary. "Modern" is a convenient name for us to give to those tendencies from which we have not yet got far enough away to view them in large masses and to describe them disinterestedly. As the blur of too close a vision extends back for us to 1870 or thereabout, we find it wise to let our romantic period, about which we can theorize and form hypotheses, end there for the present. But it already seems clear enough that the prevalent tendency even in contemporary music is still the personal and subjective one that distinguished the early romantic period. Probably our grandchildren will extend that period from Beethoven's later works to those of some composer yet unborn. And thus we have, in studying the romantic composers, the added interest that we are in a very real sense studying ourselves.

II

If, with a view to getting a more precise notion of the new tendencies, we ask ourselves now what are the salient differences between a classical and a romantic or modern piece of music, we shall be likely to notice at once certain traits of the latter, striking enough, which are nevertheless incidental rather than essential to romanticism, and must be discounted before we can come at its inmost nature. These changes have come chiefly as a result of the general evolution of musical resources, and though necessarily modifying the romantic methods, are not primary causes or effects of them. Thus, for example, the nineteenth century has seen an extraordinary development in the mechanism of all musical instruments, and in the skilful use of them by musicians. This is impressed upon us by the most cursory glance at any modern orchestral score. Haydn's and Mozart's orchestra consisted of a nucleus of strings, with a few pairs of wood and brass wind instruments added casually for solos or to reënforce certain voices in the harmonic tissue. The scheme was fundamentally monochromatic, however much it might be set off by bits of color here and there. By the time of Wagner the orchestra was essentially a group of several orchestras of divers colors: the addition of a third flute, of English horn to the oboe family, of bass clarinet, and of contrafagotto made each group of the wood-wind instruments capable of fairly complete harmony; the horns were increased in number from two to six or eight, the bass trumpet made possible complete chords for the trumpets, and there were four trombones and a choir of tubas. Thus, instead of having a uniform foundation, with variety merely in the trimming, the modern orchestra has complete, independent choirs of most various instruments, capable of all sorts of combination, opposition, and contrast.

The manner of writing for the orchestra changed as much as its constitution. Beethoven usually writes three- or four-part harmony for the strings, and doubles the wood and brass as seems effective. Tschaïkowsky and Wagner are apt to put an entire family of instruments on one melodic voice, another on another, a third on a third — as in the second movement of the "Symphonie Pathétique," at the point where flutes, oboes, clarinets, and bassoons sing the melody, while first and second violins and violas pick an obligato to it. In a word, much more attention is paid in the modern orchestra to richness and variety of tone-color and to an impressionistically effective disposition of the various timbres than in the classical scores.

The same tendency is observable in chamber and pianoforte music. Not only are modern composers fond of curious groupings of wind and string instruments, as in the trumpet septet of Saint-Saëns, the clarinet quintet and horn trio of Brahms, and other such works, but when they use only the four stringed instruments they combine contrasting rhythms and modes of phrasing, as well as pizzicato, the sordino, the high register of the 'cello, and other exotic devices, with an unfailing sense of color-values. Schubert is the first conspicuous example of this sort of quartet writing; Dvořák is his worthy follower. As for the piano, there is almost as much difference between the piano writing of Beethoven, so often thick, harsh, and lumpish, and the ramifying figuration of Schumann or the wide, clear arpeggiated accompaniments and flowering scale-figures of Chopin as there is between the coloring of Rembrandt and that of Monet.

All this gain in sensuous richness and technical elaboration is, however, to be considered largely as a concomitant rather than a direct result (though to some extent is was that) of the romantic movement. It was primarily merely a phase of that unparalleled material and mechanical progress so characteristic of the nineteenth century. The modern orchestra and the modern pianoforte are simply special examples of the ingenuity of that century in mechanical devices; the genius which turned the clavichord into the piano was the same as that which substituted the propeller for sails, and the electric telegraph for the lumbering mail-coach. But if this modern mechanical genius has indeed brought to the musician priceless gifts, it is still important to remember that perfected mechanisms do not account for romantic music, which might conceivably have existed without them. Instruments alone cannot make music, any more than a steam derrick can build a bridge. If we wish to seize the true spirit of the modern musical art, we must, after all, leave orchestra, and piano, and sensuous value behind, and ascertain to what use composers have turned all these resources, and to what manner of expression, embodied in what kind of forms, they have been spurred by the romantic spirit.

III

Difficult to make, and dangerous when made, as are sweeping generalizations about so many-sided a matter as the expressive character of whole schools or eras of art, there seem to be generic differences between classical and romantic expression which we can hardly

avoid remarking, and of which it is worth
while to attempt a tentative definition, especially
if we premise that it is to be suggestive rather
than absolute. The constant generality of
classical expression, and the objectivity of
attitude which it indicates in the worker,
cannot but strike the modern student, especially
if he contrasts them with the exactly opposite
features of contemporary art. The classical
masters aim, not at particularity and minuteness
of expression, but at the congruous setting
forth of certain broad types of feeling. They
are jealous of proportion, vigilant to maintain
the balance of the whole work, rigorous in
the exclusion of any single feature that might
through undue prominence distort or mar
its outlines. Their attitude toward their work
is detached, impersonal, disinterested — a purely
craftsmanlike attitude, at the furthest pole
from the passionate subjectivity of our modern
"tone-poets." J. S. Bach, for example, the
sovereign spirit of this school, is always concerned primarily with the plastic problem of
weaving his wonderful tonal patterns; we feel
that what these patterns turn out to express,

even though it be of great, and indeed often of supreme, poignancy, is in his mind quite a secondary matter. The preludes and fugues of the "Well-tempered Clavichord" are monuments of abstract beauty, rather than messages, pleas, or illustrations. And even when their emotional burden is so weighty as in the B-flat minor prelude or the B-minor fugue of the first book, it still remains general and, as it were, communal. Bach is not relieving his private mind; he is acting as a public spokesman, as a trustee of the emotion of a race or nation. This gives his utterance a scope, a dignity, a nobility, that cannot be accounted for by his merely personal character.

Haydn and Mozart illustrate the same attitude in a different department of music. Their symphonies and quartets are almost as impersonal as his preludes and fugues. The substance of all Haydn's best work is the folk-music of the Croatians, a branch of the Slavic race; its gaiety, elasticity, and ingenuousness are Slavic rather than merely Haydnish. It is true that he idealizes the music of his people, as a gifted individual will always idealize any

popular art he touches; but he remains true
to his source, and accurately representative of
it, just as the finest tree contains only those
elements which it can draw from the soil
in which it grows. Mozart, more personal
than Haydn, shares with him the aloofness, the
reticence, of classicism. What could be more
Greek, more celestially remote, than the G-
minor Symphony, or the quintet in the same
key? What could be less a detailed biography
of a hero, more an ideal sublimation of his
essential character, than the "Jupiter Symphony"? And even in such a deeply emotional
conception as the introduction to the C-major
quartet, can we label any specific emotion?
Can we point to the measures and say, "Here
is grief; here is disappointment; here is
unrequited love"?

In Beethoven we become conscious of a
gradually changing ideal of expression. There
are still themes, movements, entire works, in
which the dominant impulse is the architectonic
zeal of classicism; and there is the evidence
of the sketchbooks that this passionate individ-
ualist could subject himself to endless discipline

in the quest of pure plastic beauty. But there are other things, such as the third, fifth, and ninth symphonies, the "Egmont" and "Coriolanus" overtures, the slow movement of the G-major concerto (that profoundly pathetic dialogue between destiny and the human heart), and the later quartets, in which a novel particularity and subjectivity of utterance make themselves felt. In such works the self-forgetful artist, having his vicarious life only in the serene beauty of his creations, disappears, and Ludwig van Beethoven, bursting with a thousand emotions that must out, steps into his place and commands our attention, nobly egotistic, magnificently individual. And then there is the "Pastoral Symphony," in which he turns landscape painter, and with minutest details of bird-notes and shepherds' songs and peasants' dances delineates the external objects, as well as celebrates the inner spirit, of the countryside. These things mark the birth of romanticism.

For romanticism is, in essence, just this modern subjectivity and individualism, just this shifting of the emphasis from abstract beauty, with its undifferentiated expressiveness, to personal communication, minute interest in the uttermost detail, impassioned insistence on each emotion for itself rather than as a subordinate member in an articulate organism, and, in extreme cases, to concrete objects, persons, and scenes in the extra-musical world. Musicians since Beethoven have inclined to exploit more and more that aspect of their art which is analogous to language, even when this means neglect of the other aspect, the nearest analogue of which is to be found in sculpture, architecture, and decorative painting. The modern watchword has come to be initiative rather than obedience, originality rather than skill, individuality rather than truth to universal human nature. It is, after all, one impulse, the impulse toward specialization, that runs through all the various manifestations of the romantic spirit, and may be traced alike in the lyricism of Schubert, the fanciful whimsicality of Schumann, the picturesqueness of Mendelssohn, the introspection of Chopin, and the realism of Berlioz and Liszt.

In Schubert, the first of the out-and-out romanticists, and the eldest of them all in point of time (his birth date falls in the eighteenth century), we find a curious grafting of a new spirit on an old stem. Brought up on the quartets and symphonies of Haydn and Mozart, making his first studies in boyishly literal imitation of them, he acquired the letter of the classical idiom as none of the others save Mendelssohn ever did. His works in sonata form, written up to 1816, might well have emanated from Esterhaz or Salzburg; the C-major Symphony, so far as general plan is concerned, would have done no discredit to Beethoven. Yet the spirit of Schubert is always lyrical. It was fated from his birth that he should write songs, for his was a typically sentimental temperament; and when he planned a symphony, he instinctively conceived it as a series of songs for instruments, somewhat more developed than those intended for a voice, but hardly different in kind. As a naturalist can reconstruct in fancy an extinct animal from a fossil jaw-bone, a musical historian might piece out a fair conception of what romanticism is, in the dearth of other evidence, from a study of "Erlkönig," or "Ständchen," or "Am

Meer"; and the ideas he might thus form would be extended rather than altered by acquaintance with the "Unfinished Symphony" or the D-minor Quartet. The lyrical Schubert contrasts always with the heroic and impersonal Bach or Beethoven, much as Tennyson contrasts with Shakspere, or Theocritus with Sophocles.

Schumann adds to the lyrical ardor of Schubert insatiable youthful enthusiasm, whimsicality, a richly poetic fancy, and a touch of mysticism. His songs are even more personal than Schubert's, and his piano pieces, especially the early ones, bristle with eccentricities. The particularity, minute detail, and personal connotation of the "Abegg Variations," the "Davidsbündertänze," the "Papillons," the "Carnaval," the "Kreisleriana," are almost grotesque. He confides to us, through this music, his friendships, his flirtations, his courtship, his critical sympathies, his artistic creed, his literary devotions. Never was music so circumstantial, so autobiographic. In later years, when he had passed out of the enchanted circle of youthful egotism, and was striving for a more universal speech, his point of view became not essentially less personal but only less wayward. Till the last his art is vividly self-conscious — that is his charm and his limitation. No one has so touchingly voiced the aspirations of the imprisoned soul, no one has put meditation and introspection into tones, as he has done in the adagio of the C-major Symphony, the " Funeral March" of the Quintet, the F-sharp major Romance for piano.

If Schumann sounds, as no other can, the whole gamut of feeling of a sensitive modern soul, Mendelssohn, quite dissimilar in temperament, — correct, reserved, dispassionate, — is nevertheless also romantic by virtue of his picturesqueness, his keen sense for the pageantry of life, his delicate skill as an illustrator of nature and of imaginative literature. His "Songs without Words" reveal a strain of mild lyricism, but he is never intimate or reckless, he never wholly reveals himself. His discreet objectivity is far removed from the frankly subjective enthusiasms of Schubert and Schumann. He was, in fact, by tradition, training, and native taste, a classicist; the exhibition of deep feeling was distasteful to his fastidious reticence;

and he is thus emotionally less characteristic of his period than any of his contemporaries. But for all that he shows unmistakably in the felicity of his tone-painting the modern interest in picturesque detail, in the concrete circumstance, the significant particular. Illustration rather than abstract beauty — that is one of the special interests of the new school. No one has cultivated it more happily than the composer of the "Midsummer Night's Dream" music, the "Hebrides Overture," and the "Scotch" and "Italian" Symphonies.

Chopin presents an even more singular instance than Schumann affords of what introspection can make of a composer, of how resolute self-communion can individualize his work until its intense personal savor keeps little to remind us of other music. All Chopin's tastes were so aristocratic that the exclusiveness of his style seems a matter of course, and was probably to his mind a supreme merit. And if it debarred him from some musical experiences, if it made his music sound better in a drawing-room than in a concert hall, it certainly gave it a marvellous delicacy, finesse, originality,

and fragile beauty. It is, so to speak, vale-
tudinarian music, and preserves its pure white
complexion only by never venturing into the full
sunlight. Here, then, is another differentiation in musical style, a fresh departure from
the classic norm, due to the exacting taste of
the mental aristocrat, the carefully self-bounded
dreamer and sybarite.

Markedly specialized as the expression is,
however, in Schubert, Schumann, Mendelssohn,
and Chopin, and strikingly contrasted as it is
with the serene generality of the classical
music, the two schools after all differ rather in
the degree of emphasis they lay on the various
elements of effect than in kind. Both, we feel,
are using the same means, though to such
different ends. But with Berlioz and Liszt
we pass into a new world, in which not only
emphasis and intention, but the actual materials
and the fundamental principles of art, have
undergone a change. These men have pushed
the romantic concreteness even beyond the
range of sentiments and emotions, to invade
that of facts and events. They are no longer
satisfied with the minutiæ of feelings; they

must depict for us the external appearance of the people who feel, give us not only heroes, but these heroes' coats, with the exact number of buttons and the proper cut, according to the fashion of the particular decade. If Schumann and his fellows are the sentimental novelists of music, the Thackerays and the George Eliots, here are the naturalists, the scientific analysts, the "realists" with microscope and scalpel in hand, the Zolas and the Gorkys.

This insistence on the letter is quite instinctive with Berlioz. In the first place, he was a Frenchman; and the French have a genius for the concrete, and in music have shown their bias by approaching it always from the dramatic, histrionic point of view. Opera is the norm of music to the Frenchman. For him, music originates in the opera-house, quite as inevitably as for the German it originates in the concert room. Berlioz's "symphonies," therefore, as a matter of course, took the form of operas, with the characters and action suppressed or relegated to the imagination.

In the second place, the active impulses in Berlioz's personal temperament predominated over the contemplative to a degree unusual even in his countrymen; he conceived a work of art in terms not of emotion but of action; and his musical thinking was a sort of narration in tones. He accordingly wrote, with ingenuous spontaneity, in a style that was, from the German standpoint, revolutionary, unprecedented, iconoclastic — a style the essence of which was its matter-of-fact realism. His "Symphonie Fantastique," which Mr. Hadow calls his most uncompromising piece of program music, sets forth the adventures of a hero (whose identity with the composer is obvious) in five movements or acts, and with the most sedulous particularity. We first see him struggling with love, tormented by jealousy, consoled by religion; then in a ball-room, pausing in the midst of the dance to muse on his beloved; then in the country, listening to idyllic shepherds and hearing the summer thunder. He dreams that he has murdered the beloved, that he is to be beheaded at the guillotine; he is surrounded by witches, his mistress has herself become a witch, the *Dies Iræ* clangs its knell of death across the wild chaos of the dance. . . .

Now in all this the striking point is the concreteness of the imagery, the plenitude of detail, the narrative and descriptive literalness of the treatment — and above all the subordination of the music to a merely symbolic function. Berlioz here brings into prominence for the first time the device, so frequent in later operatic and program music, of treating his themes or motives as symbols of his characters, associated with these by a purely arbitrary but nevertheless effective bond. When we hear the melody we are expected to think of the character, and all the changes rung on it are prompted not by the desire for musical development, but by psychological considerations connected with the dramatic action. Thus, for example, in this symphony the motive known as "*l'idée fixe*" represents the beloved; its fragmentary appearances in the second, third, and fourth movements tell us that the thought of her is passing through our hero's mind; and in the last movement, when she endues the horrid form of a witch, we hear a distorted, grotesque version of it sardonically whistled by the piccolo. Highly characteristic

25

of Berlioz is this use of melodies, so dearly valued in classic music for themselves alone, as mere counters for telling off the incidents in the plot, or cues for the entrances of the *dramatis personæ*.

Liszt, a man of keener musical perception than Berlioz, placed himself also, in obedience to his strong dramatic sense, on the same artistic platform. In such a work as the "Faust Symphony" we discern a more musical nature producing practically the same kind of music. There is the same narrative and descriptive intention; the three movements take their names from the chief characters in the action, Faust, Gretchen, and Mephistopheles; and though the second is more general in expression than Berlioz ever is, the other two are good examples of his method. There is also the same machinery of leading motives and their manipulation according to the requirements of symbolism, even to the parodying of the Faust themes in the "Mephistopheles" section. In the symphonic poem, "Les Préludes," however (and in the "Dante Symphony" and other compositions),

Liszt shows his German blood in a treatment more imaginative, the actuating subjects being often not persons and events, but emotional and mental states. But the fact that many of the transformations of the themes are from the musical standpoint travesties, justified only by their psychological intention, shows that the attitude even here is still that of the dramatist, not that of the abstract musician. The art, in a word, is still representative, not presentative and self-sufficing. Again, the representative function of music for Liszt is shown by his tendency to approach composition indirectly, and through extraneous interests of his many-sided mind, instead of with the classic single-mindedness: his pieces are suggested by natural scenery, historical characters, philosophic abstractions, poems, novels, and even statues and pictures.

In all these ways and degrees we see exemplified the inclination of the nineteenth-century composers to seek a more and more definite, particular, and concrete type of expression. Subjective shades and nuances take the place of the ground-colors of classicism;

music comes to have so personal a flavor that it is as impossible to confound a piece of Chopin with one of Schumann as it is difficult, by internal evidence alone, to say whether Mozart or Haydn is the author of an unfamiliar symphony; ultimately, insistence upon special emotions opens the way to absorption in what is even more special — individual characters, events, and situations, — and on the heels of the lyrical treads the realistic. The artistic stream thus reverses the habit of natural streams: as it gets farther and farther from its source it subdivides and subdivides itself again, until it is no longer a single large body, but a multitude of isolated brooks and rivulets. Our contemporary music, unlike the classical, is not the expression of a single social consciousness, but rather a heterogeneous aggregate of the utterances of many individuals. What is most captivating about it is the sensitive fidelity with which it reflects its composers' idiosyncrasies.

IV

All things human, however, have their price, and romanticism is no exception to the rule. The composers of the romantic period, in becoming more particular, grew in the same proportion less universal; in bowing to the inexorable evolutionary force that makes each modern man a specialist, they inevitably sacrificed something of the breadth, the catholicity, the magnanimity, of the old time. It is doubtless a sense of some such loss as this, dogging like a shadow all our gains, that takes us back periodically to a new appreciation of the classics. There is often a feeling of relief, of freer breathing and ampler leisure, as when we leave the confusion of the city for the large peace of the country, in turning from the modern complexities to the old simplicities, and forgetting that there is any music but Bach's. The reasons for this contrast between the two schools must of course lie deeply hidden in the psychology of æsthetics, but a clew to them at least may be found near at hand, in the conditions of life, the everyday environments, of the two groups of artists.

It has often been remarked that the composers of the nineteenth century have been men of more cultivation, of greater intellectual elasticity and resulting breadth of interest, than their predecessors. Palestrina, Bach, Handel, Haydn, Mozart, even Beethoven, concentrating their whole minds on music, were far less curious as to other human pursuits than their later brethren. The six composers we are studying are impressive instances of this modern many-sidedness of mind. At least three of them, Schumann, Berlioz, and Liszt, were skilled journalists and men of letters; Schumann with the finely judicial, fancifully conceived sketches of his *New Journal of Music*, Berlioz with his brilliant, fantastically humorous feuilletons, and Liszt with his propaganda, in book and pamphlet, of Wagner, Chopin, and other contemporaries. (Fancy Bach interrupting his steady stream of cantatas to write an exposition of the genius of Handel!) Schumann was, moreover, something of a poet, and Mendelssohn was one of the most voluminous and picturesque of letter-writers. Chopin was as versed in social as in musical graces and Liszt was — what was he not? — a courtier, a Lovelace, a man of the world, and an abbé. Schubert alone, of them all the eldest and the nearest to classical traditions, was a composer pure and simple.

The versatility of these men was no accident or freak of coincidence; it was the effective trait that made their work so profusely allusive, so vividly minute, in short, so romantic. And what is more to our purpose just here, it was the underlying cause of a defect which is quite as symptomatic of romanticism as its merits. So various a mental activity must needs lack something in depth; if attention is spread wide it must be spread thin; thought given to avocations must be borrowed from the vocation. We should expect to find, accordingly, division of energy resulting, here as elsewhere, in a lack of concentration, a failure of power; and herein we are not disappointed. With the possible exception of Mendelssohn, no one of our six composers can compare, simply as a handicraftsman, with Bach or Mozart.

Schubert was so little a contrapuntist that he had just engaged lessons when death interrupted his brief career. Schumann and Chopin gave in their youth innumerable hours that should have counted for systematic to routine the fanciful improvisation so seductive to poetic temperaments. Berlioz kicked down all the fences in his coltish days, and ever after looked askance at the artistic harness. Liszt, for all his diabolical cleverness, remained the slave of mannerisms, and became a dupe of his own rhetorical style.

Now there is doubtless in all this waywardness something that strikes in us a chord such as vibrates in sympathy with the small boy who, regardless of barbed wire, invades the orchard and carries off the delectable green apples. It is a fine thing to be young, it is glorious to be free. But sober second thought relentlessly follows: we know that apples must be sent to market in due course, and that that exciting green fruit is, after all, indigestible and unripe; and we know equally that musicians must undergo their apprenticeship, and that all art executed without adequate

technical mastery is crude. The crudity of
the art of our musical orchard-robbers becomes
at once evident when we compare a single
melody, or an entire movement, of Schubert or
his successors with one by Mozart or Beethoven.

The single melody is the molecule of music,
the smallest element in it that cannot be sub-
divided without loss of character. Every great
melody has an indefinable distinction, a sort
of personal flavor or individuality, which we
may discern but cannot analyze. It has also,
however, an organic quality, depending upon both
the unity and the variety of its phraseology,
that we can to a certain extent study and define.
Assuming, to start with, the subtle distinction
without which it would sink into the commonplace, we can compare and contrast it with
other melodies in respect of its organic quality,
its simultaneous presentation of unity and
variety — in a word, its plastic beauty. Such
a melody as the second theme of the first
movement of Mozart's G-minor Quintet,
for example, gains a wonderful charm from the
complexity, and at the same time the final

simplicity, of its phrase structure. The several musical figures, or motives, of which it is composed follow each other without the least impression of crass mechanical dovetailing; yet one feels, as they proceed, such a sense of logical progression, of orderly sequence, that the final cadence seems like an audible "Q. E. D." Contrasted with such dexterous phrase-weaving as this, many of Schubert's and Schumann's tunes, with their literal repetitions of short phrases, their set thesis and antithesis, seem pitifully bald and trite. It is hardly fair to take extreme cases, but they best bring out the point. Schubert's "Drang in die Ferne," ten consecutive measures of which repeat literally the same rhythm, and the theme in Schumann's "Abegg Variations," in which a single phrase recurs sixteen times, will make it almost painfully evident. This tendency to rhythmic monotony, to an unvaried singsong re-iteration of phrase, besets constantly these two composers, too often takes Chopin in its grasp, and in Mendelssohn is aggravated by an inclination to stay in one key, page after page, until our heads droop with drowsiness. Berlioz, on the other hand, errs in the opposite direction. Variety, with him, degenerates into a chaotic miscellaneousness, and what should be an agreeably diversified landscape becomes a pathless jungle. In both cases there is a failure of the constructive faculty, due to a lack of mental coördination and concentration. The price paid for interesting detail is monotony or instability in the organism.

Similar weaknesses reveal themselves when we pass from considering the elemental melodies to survey the ways in which they are built up into larger sections and whole movements — when we pass, that is, from form to structure.[1] None of the romantic composers attained a breadth, diversity, and solidity of construction in any wise comparable to Beethoven's. Schubert was intellectually too indolent, if not

[1] Properly speaking, "form" refers to the molecular constitution of music, to the ways in which relations of pitch and rhythm are manipulated in melody and harmony; "structure" to the molar constitution of music, the subsequent grouping of the melodies into complete pieces. The difference between a sonata, a fugue, and a nocturne is a difference of structure; the difference between a good melody and a bad one is a difference of form.

indifferent, to attempt intricate syntheses of his materials, but relied instead on their primitive charm to justify endless repetitions. Schumann, less tolerant of platitude, and gifted with more intense, if hardly more disciplined, imagination, resorted to constant kaleidoscopic change, resulting in those "mosaic forms" which are related to true cyclic forms much as a panorama is related to a picture. Mendelssohn was naturally a better master of construction, but the knots he ties are somewhat loose and inclined to ravel out. Chopin, a born miniaturist, obviously fails to make his sonatas and concertos anything but chance bundles of lyrical pieces. As for Berlioz and Liszt, they frankly faced their dilemma, and had the shrewdness to disclaim the desire to do that for which they wanted the faculty. They fell back on the "poetic forms," and let their works pile up without internal coherence, held together only by the thread of the story they were illustrating.

For this failure to work out the highest degree of plastic beauty possible to them, the romanticists frequently have to pay in a serious loss of power. Keenly interesting as are the details of their work, the whole impression is apt to lack fusion, clearness, integrity. Not without terrible risks may the musician neglect form, since form is itself, for him, perhaps more than for any of his brother artists in other mediums, a fundamental means of expression. Of this matter popular thought is inclined to take a superficial view; it is fond of confusing vital form with dry formalism, of speaking contemptuously of formal analysis as the pedantic dissection of lovely melodies, the plucking and counting of the petals of the flowers of art, and of reiterating *ad nauseam* its irritating half-truth, "Music is the language of the emotions." Popular thought would do well to pause and consider; to ask itself whether language too has not its form, without which it is unintelligible; to inquire how much of the expressive power of a lovely melody would remain were its pitch and time relations (that is, its form) materially altered, how long we could be inspired by the most exciting rhythms, were they ceaselessly reiterated without relief, and how eloquent we should find even the most moving symphony, were it written all in one key, or in several keys that had no relation to one another. Such consideration soon suggests the truth, which impresses us the more the more deeply we study music, that there is a general expressiveness underlying all particular expressions, a fundamental beauty by which all special beauties are nourished as flowers are nourished by the soil, a symmetry and orderly organization that can no more be dispensed with in music without crippling its eloquence than a normal regularity of the features can be dispensed with in the human face without distorting it into absurdity or debasing it into ugliness. Without its pervasive presence, all special features, however amusing or superficially appealing, fail to inspire or charm. They become as wild flowers plucked to languish indoors, as seaweeds taken from their natural setting of liquid coolness. Or again, the particular expressions of music may be compared to the strings of an instrument, of which the sounding board is plastic beauty; without its sympathetic reënforcement the strings, strike them as we may, give forth a scarcely audible murmur; with it, there is clear and powerful sonority. So the most ingenious music is dull and dead if it lack the vitality of organic form, but if it be beautiful it will make its way directly to the heart.

It is surely not necessary to add that this discussion of the primal importance of form is not intended to impeach all romantic music as deficient in the appeal that beauty alone can make. This were indeed a *reductio ad absurdum*. Much of the music of Schubert, Schumann, Mendelssohn, and Chopin is of the rarest beauty, and, by the same token, of the most moving eloquence. The intention of our analysis is rather to secure that aid to the appreciation of just such beauties which discrimination alone can give, and by means of comparison to sharpen the focus of our mental image of what romanticism achieves and of what it fails to achieve. At its best, we shall rejoice to find, it shares the serene loveliness, the impersonal grandeur, of classicism. At its less than best, it offers us a vivid intellectual interest, a keen pleasure in following its wide ramifications and its faithful illustrations of many phases of life. At its worst only does its exaggerated passion for detail mislead it into petty and prosaic literalism.

V

A slightly different angle of approach to this whole problem of musical expression is afforded by psychological analysis. Here, again, as we might expect, modern theory, the learned as well as the popular, is somewhat biassed by the prominence in modern practice of certain special features of effect. The psychologists dwell with a pardonable partiality of vision on the means of special expression; to complete their theories the reader has often to add for himself a consideration of the psychology of form. An article by M. Edmond Goblot, entitled "La Musique Descriptive,"[1] is interesting, like others of its kind, both for what it explains and for what it ignores.

M. Goblot classifies expressive music under three headings, to which he gives the names of "*la musique emotive*," "*la musique descriptive*," and "*la musique imitative*." His first rubric

[1] *La Revue Philosophique*, Vol. LII.

is somewhat vague, a sort of rag-bag into which he stuffs *"toute musique qui provoque l'emotion sans aucun intermediaire conscient."* The other two are not only more precise, but serve to call attention to devices which have become very prominent in romantic, and especially in modern realistic, music. "Imitative" music, by reproducing literally sounds heard in the extra-musical world of nature, suggests to the listener the objects and events associated with them. Examples are the bird-notes in Beethoven's "Pastoral Symphony," the thunder in Berlioz's "Symphonie Fantastique," the bleating of sheep in Strauss's "Don Quixote," the striking of the clock and the wailing of the baby in his "Symphonia Domestica." "Descriptive" music suggests actions and events by means of analogies, chiefly of movement and of utterance, between the music and the object, and is of course far commoner than the more literal and narrowly circumscribed imitation. Beethoven is descriptive when he represents the even flowing of the brook, in the "Pastoral Symphony," by rippling figures in eighth notes, or when in the bass recitatives of the

Ninth Symphony he suggests the impassioned utterance of an imaginary protagonist; Mendelssohn describes in his "Hebrides Overture" the heaving of the ocean, and in his "Midsummer Night's Dream" the dancing of fairies; Saint-Saëns reproduces in "Le Rouet d'Omphale" the very whirr of the spinning-wheel, and Wagner in his fire-music the ceaseless lapping of flames.

Such devices as these certainly occupy a prominent place in modern music. Almost every composer of the later nineteenth century has taken his fling at this sort of sketching from nature. One cannot resist, nevertheless, the suspicion that M. Goblot attaches too great an importance to what is, after all, a casual and desultory element in most compositions, and that he inclines to lay on the narrow shoulders of imitation and description a greater burden of explanation than they can carry. Beethoven's birds and brooks are attractive features in a great work; Saint-Saëns' spinning-wheel makes a charming arabesque on a harmony of solid musicianship; but what are we to say to M. Goblot's assertion that a passage cited from Alexandre George, modulating upward by whole steps, is emphatically expressive because it "reminds us of a person reiterating with growing exaltation the same authoritative or impassioned affirmation, and each time advancing a step, in an attitude of menace or defiance"? Can we accept as unquestioningly as he does a series of thirteen consecutive fifths, descriptive of sunrise, on the ground that it "wounds our ears as the light of the sun wounds our eyes"? And listen to his comment on Schubert's "Trout," that long-suffering denizen of Teutonic waters: *"En courant sur son lit de pierres, elle se creuse de plis profonds, se hérisse de crêtes saillantes, et ces plis et ces crêtes se croisent obliquement en miroitant."* Schubert's fat shoulders, we suspect, would have shaken could he have read this ingenious commentary on his work.

If such finical transcription of natural sights and sounds is the aim of music, why do we prefer Beethoven's thunder, which clings cravenly to the diatonic scale, to Berlioz's, so much more realistic in its daring dissonance? Why do we not forthwith turn about face on the road our art has so long been travelling, and forsake musical intervals, those quite artificial figments, for the noises which surround us everywhere in the actual world? Noise is indeed the hidden goal toward which all description and imitation aspire, and sound could never have passed into music under their guidance, but only in quest of a far deeper, more subtle expressiveness. It is hard to believe that any sane listener would long continue to patronize music in which there was not something more truly satisfying than the lapping of brooks, the crashing of storm or battle, and the whirring of spinning-wheels or the creaking of wind-mills. If such were the case, we should have to admit sadly that music had fallen to the level to which dramatic art falls in the real-tank-and-practicable-saw-mill melodrama, to which painting falls in those pictures from which we try to pluck the too tangible grape.

M. Goblot evidently realizes himself that there is a subtler appeal than that of description and imitation; for it is in order to account for it that he makes his separate heading of "*la musique emotive*," by which he indicates all music which acts directly upon the emotions, without the aid of any recognition of external objects, any intellectual concepts, or, as he says, "*aucun intermediaire conscient.*" The appeal he here has in mind is that of thousands of melodies, which, without describing or imitating any concrete object, suggest vividly special states of feeling, by recalling to us, in veiled, modified, and idealized form, those gestures or cries we habitually make under the spur of such feelings. Since the spontaneous vocal expressions of strong emotion — wailing, crying, pleading, moaning, and the like — have all their characteristic cadences, which can be more or less accurately reproduced in a bit of melody, and since the natural bodily gesticulations can be similarly suggested by divers rhythmical movements, music has the power to induce a great variety of emotional states by what we may call direct contagion, without the intermediation of any mental images. It can act upon us like the infection of tears or laughter, to which we involuntarily succumb, without asking for any reasons. And it certainly exercises this power much more constantly and steadily than it imitates or describes. Almost all lyrical melodies, such as Schumann's "Ich Grolle Nicht," with its persistently rising inflection of earnest protestation, or Chopin's "Funeral March," with its monotone of heavy grief, will be found on analysis to reëcho, in an idealized and transfigured form, the natural utterance of passion. This kind of expression, which has been frequently described, appeals to our subconscious associations rather than to those conscious processes of thought by which we follow realistic delineation. Operating at a deeper level in our natures, it is proportionately more potent and irresistible.

But is even this type of expression, more general and pervasive though it be than the types so interestingly studied by M. Goblot — is even this style of expression universal, omnipresent, fundamental? Does it suffice to explain the overwhelming emotional appeal of an organ-fugue of Bach, for example, of which the impression seems to be vague, general, indefinable in specific terms, in the exact measure of its profundity? If "*la musique emotive*" works at a deeper level and upon a more subconscious element in our nature than *"la musique imitative"* and *"la musique descriptive,"* is there not still another kind of music, which we may perhaps best call simply *"la musique belle,"* which, addressing still deeper instincts, exercises an even more magical persuasiveness?

The case of the Bach fugue forces us to the conclusion that there is indeed a kind of expression depending neither on the portrayal of natural objects nor on the suggestion of such special feelings as joy and grief, but penetrating by a still deeper avenue to the primal springs of our emotion. The more compelling the experience, it seems, the more is it idealized away from concrete references and provocations in the direction of abstract musical beauty. By presenting to us a perfect piece of form, a highly complex yet ultimately single organism of tones, it calls into full play our most fudamental perceptions; and this satisfying exercise of our faculties gives us a pervasive happiness, a diffused sense of efficient vitality, ineffably more delightful than any particularized emotion or isolated intellectual process. Perfection of form thus turns out to be the most indispensable of all the means of expression at the command of the composer.

Psychological analysis, carried to its legitimate end, verifies, we see, the conclusions of the naïve musical observer. All expression, for psychology, is the product of an association between two "terms" in the mind—the first that which is given by experience, the expressive object, the second that system of thoughts and feelings at which the mind arrives through the associative act, that which, as we say, is expressed. This being the case, it is evident that, other things being equal, that expression will be most potent the first term of which most deeply stirs our instinctive, subconscious life. When the first term is a basic activity of our minds, such as the perception of a beautiful form, the feelings to which it leads us will have a peculiar depth and amplitude. Our whole organism, like the sounding-board of the well-attuned instrument, will be set in vibration. This is what happens when we listen sympathetically to music that is really beautiful. When, on the other hand, the mental trigger pulled is only some special emotion, so that the stimulation is superficial or local, the impression will reverberate less far-reachingly. We shall be less profoundly moved. And when it is not even an emotion, however special, that starts off the train of thought, but the intellectual concept of some object or event, we shall likely be not so much moved as interested; our curiosity rather than our passions will respond; and we shall call the music bizarre, original, or striking, but hardly beautiful. Something like the same gradation in the power of various appeals, according to their generality, is observable in ordinary life. To read a love-story, labyrinthine in minute detail, is a less seizing experience than to overhear the impassioned speech of some actual lover, even if we catch none of the words; and this in turn commoves us less than to feel in our own frames that boiling of the blood, that surging of the vitals, which is the raw material of love. Brisk exercise on a fine autumn day of sun and wind gives a richer happiness than is dreamed of in our philosophies. It communicates no particular ideas, but attunes our whole being so exquisitely that the fancies spring up spontaneously, like wild-flowers in a fertile meadow. So lovely music simply establishes in us a mood, leaving all the furniture of that mood to our imaginations. And this is why it is that artistic expression, as it becomes more minute and meticulously precise, is apt to lose in persuasive power, and that the composer, if he understands his medium, must needs hesitate long before sacrificing the least degree of beauty, however interstitial and inconspicuous, to any isolated feature of interest, no matter how salient or seductive.

VI

Perhaps it is not too much to hope that the foregoing analysis, incomplete and tentative as it is, affords us something like a rational basis for our instinctive attitudes toward the various types of music. Though its intention is to suggest rather than to dogmatize, it may by this time have fixed clearly in our minds certain fundamental principles of artistic effect; and by constant reference to these it may have established in us a measure of judicial impartiality and poise. Especially, it may have clarified our notions, likely to remain confused so long as they are unconscious, of the essential achievements of the romantic school, both in its lyrical and in its realistic phases, as well as of the peculiar drawbacks and limitations to which it is subject.

The abiding charm of the lyrical work of the romantic composers, typical of which are Schubert's songs, Schumann's novelettes and *phantasiestücke*, and Chopin's nocturnes and preludes, lies in its intimateness, its strong personal flavor. It fascinates us by its impulsive self-revelation, its frankness, spontaneity, and enthusiasm. Its subjectivity and introspection, even when they are troubled or touched with sadness, stir a sympathetic chord in the self-conscious modern breast. To those moods which the classic reticence chills and repels, romantic music speaks with tender, caressing humanity. Even its limitations are then an added appeal; for when we are too weary or dull to brace ourselves to the perception of impersonal beauty, the accent of private grief, aspiration, struggle, and disappointment seems better pitched to our capacity, and has a pathos we can understand. Schumann and Chopin are the best companions for hours of reverie and self-communion. On the other hand, when those hours overtake us in which we realize the pathetic incompleteness of all merely personal life, in which we discern what fragmentary creatures we are, and how little of truth we can ever see, then all living to ourselves alone is touched with the sense of vanity. Then every utterance of our petty private griefs, and even of our nobler but still private joys, seems like a breath dissipated in a universe; we find true existence, solid reality, only in an identification of our interests with those of all mankind. As morals finds its escape from this sense of the vanity of individual living in social devotion, æsthetics finds it in the impersonality of classic art. Romanticism is sometimes silent, or speaks to unattending ears. We turn from all special expressions, touched as they are with human mortality and evanescence, to the eternal abstract beauty.

If lyrical music is unsatisfactory to these moods of highest vitality and severest demand, realistic music is exasperating, intolerable. When we have nothing better to do it is amusing enough to note the ingenuity with which a composer can introduce the bray of an ass into his delicate tissue of tones, as Mendelssohn does in the "Midsummer Night's Dream Overture," or make three bird-notes sound a harmonic triad as Beethoven does in his "Pastoral Symphony." There is a fascinating technical problem involved in the suggestion of natural noises by musical tones, and when we are indifferent to such technical interests, we may still find diversion in following a series of tonal cues to the events of a familiar story. But when we crave the sublimity of music, when we long to feel once more the thrill of its transcendent beauty, how can we endure to be put off with the barking of a dog, the mewing of a cat, the galloping of a horse, or the crying of a baby? Most program music is incredibly trivial in intention, and gives an impression of maladaptation of means to ends, the former are so elaborate, the latter so paltry and

53

mean. To elicit from a modern orchestra of a hundred instruments a feeble imitation of a battle seems, as some one has piquantly phrased it, "like using a steam-hammer to kill a fly."

We read with impatience the annals of this school. John Mundy, an English composer of the seventeenth century, writes a "Fantasia on the Weather," in four parts: "Faire Weather; Lightning; Thunder; a Faire Day." Adam Krieger, in 1667, composes a four-part vocal fugue "entirely imitative of cats," on a chromatic subject set to the words "Miau, miau." Dussek produces a series of pieces entitled "The Sufferings of the Queen of France," some of which are: "The Queen's Imprisonment" (*largo*); "She reflects on her Former Greatness" (*maestoso*); "Her Invocation to the Almighty just before her Death" (*devotamente*); "The Guillotine drops" (a *glissando* descending scale); "Apotheosis." We smile patronizingly over these first childish attempts of an art essentially childish. No longer satisfied with such innocent delineations of natural and political history, we must have autobiography, domesticity, and even metaphysics, translated into tones.

But will posterity take a truly keener delight in our triumphs of realism than we do in the works of Mundy and Krieger? Already Mr. Arthur Symons, in his essay on Richard Strauss, cries in pardonable irritation: "If I cared more for literature than for music, I imagine that I might care greatly for Strauss. He offers me sound as literature. But I prefer to read my literature, and to hear nothing but music."

Were triviality the only sin of program music we might leave it, without further ado, to the gradual oblivion which overtakes the jejune in art. But, unfortunately, program music not merely bores the music-lover; it does him a positive injury, which criticism ought, so far as it can, to mitigate. By its false emphasis it distracts attention from what music can do supremely to what it can only botch and bungle, brings true masterpieces into discredit with hearers not sensitive or disciplined enough to appreciate them, and plunges the simple into a hopeless æsthetic quagmire. Pitiable is the frequency of such questions, on the lips of aspiring students, as, "Ought I, when I listen to music, to have in mind a series of

pictures, or a story?" To judge by the minuteness of its detail the art which beyond all
others is great by virtue of indefinite suggestion,
and inspires by appealing to faculties far below
the level of intellectual consciousness, is to be
sadly duped. "We forget," writes Vernon Lee,
"that music is neither a symbol which can
convey an abstract thought, nor a brute cry
which can express an instinctive feeling; we
wish to barter the power of leaving in the mind
an indelible image of beauty for the miserable
privilege of awakening the momentary recollection of one of nature's sounds, or the yet
more miserable one of sending a momentary
tremor through the body; we would rather
compare than enjoy, and rather weep than
admire."

The upshot of all this is, that not even in
enjoying the novel delights, the picturesque
glimpses, and the fancy-provoking allusiveness
which romanticism has introduced into music
should we give ourselves too unreservedly to
what may be, after all, but a partial and limited
pleasure. If these things make us indifferent
to deeper beauties they do us a disservice. If,

however, we can keep, in spite of their seductions, our sense of proportion, our perception of relative values, we shall enjoy them in security. The romantic movement has undoubtedly led to a widening of our artistic sympathies, has enriched our music with new expressive possibilities and technical resources. It has been one of those periods of ebullience, corresponding perhaps in the consciousness of the race to the storm and stress of adolescence in the individual, which are bound to come so long as we are growing. We cannot fully maintain our poise at the very moment in which we are extending our field of experience; periods of conquest must alternate with periods of assimilation; and as in walking we constantly lose our balance in order to progress, so in mental life we willingly forego control until it can supervene on a broader consciousness.

The romantic composers, eagerly developing the expressive possibilities of music, may have forgotten sometimes in their enthusiasm the organic beauty without which music can never wholly satisfy, but nevertheless they have enriched their art. The available resources of music are to-day more various than ever before. Not only have its mechanical facilities been wonderfully perfected by the ingenuity of the nineteenth century, but its potentialities for vivid and detailed expression have been permanently raised by the subjective intentness of the modern temperament. It remains for future composers to make a new synthesis of all these novel elements, and without sacrificing their vividness to impose upon them the ultimate integrity of impression which at present they too often lack. A classical unity and beauty must supervene upon our romantic multiplicity and interesting confusion. Expression, without losing the minuteness that modern speculation has gained for it, must regain something of the classical serenity. We have had already one musician who, profiting by his heritage, has vied with Schumann in versatility and with Bach in intimacy, who has combined in his single mind something of the sensitive sympathy of the romanticists and the rugged power of the classicists. It may be that Brahms but points the way to a music of the future which will be as grand as it is vivid, as universal in scope as it is personal in accent and inspiration, and in which beauty of form and richness of expression will be reunited in perfect coöperation to one great artistic end.

II
FRANZ SCHUBERT

FRANZ SCHUBERT
From an original water color by W. A. Rieder

FRANZ SCHUBERT

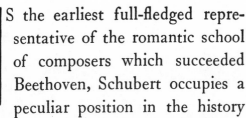

S the earliest full-fledged representative of the romantic school
of composers which succeeded
Beethoven, Schubert occupies a
peculiar position in the history
of music. His work forms the link between
the classical music of Haydn, Mozart, and
Beethoven and the romantic music of Schumann, Mendelssohn, and Chopin, having certain
qualities in common with each. Traditions,
training, and environment allied him with the
older order; but instinct led him into new
paths. Scattered plentifully through the thousands of pages covered by his racing pen, many
of which might be the work of some humdrum
eighteenth-century kapellmeister, are features
of surprising novelty, pointing unmistakably to
the future rather than to the past—gleams of
the true gold in a vast heap of sand. Nine-

tenths of the time he is content to imitate, with amiable, unthinking garrulity, the quartets and sonatas he grew up with; the other tenth he breaks forth incontinently, an inspired pioneer. This mingling of the matter-of-course and the unexpected, of the sand and the gold, makes his music a curious study.

Born in Vienna, January 31, 1797, Schubert began the study of music when still a child, under the direction of his father, a school-teacher by profession, and his two brothers. While in his teens the boy began playing the viola parts in the family string quartet. His brothers took the violin parts, and his father played the 'cello: not always impeccably, it is to be feared, for we read how little Franz, look-ing doubtless very solemn and gnomelike in the spectacles he already wore, would from time to time, without stopping to look at the score, comment on the wrong notes the paternal fingers were sounding. This informal quartet was the nucleus of an orchestra, known as the Orchestral Society of Amateurs, which flourished at a somewhat later period, and served to make Schubert acquainted with the works of Krommer, Romberg, Cherubini, Spontini, Câtel, Mehul, Boieldieu, Weigl, Winter, and others of that category, as well as with some Haydn and Mozart, and the first two symphonies of Beethoven. There was also an orchestra in the government school for the Emperor's choir, known as the "Convict" (from *convivo*, not *convinco*), which the boy, thanks to his clear soprano voice, attended from his eleventh to his sixteenth year; and of this he was not only a member, but for some time a conductor. One can readily imagine that with all this music-making there was little time for general schooling. Indeed, from the moment he left the Convict, in 1813, he seems to have given little thought to any but a technical education; and though he attended a normal school for a while, and later even tried teaching under his father for three years, his main interests were his lessons with the famous opera composer, Salieri, and his first essays in composition.

For the instinct of imitation had started him composing at an age when most boys nowadays are learning arithmetic. At thirteen he broke the ice with a four-hand piano fantasia, and from that moment swam contentedly through a sea of manuscripts. His teeming fecundity and his carelessness for the children of his brain once they were hatched showed themselves from the first. When he mislaid thirty minuets written at the Convict, he would not trouble to recopy them; what he enjoyed was the activity, not its product; and it was dull to bottle old water while the spring was flowing so cool and fresh. The figure of a spring does scant justice to Schubert's inexhaustible fancy; it was more like one of those magic knapsacks in the fairy stories — the more he took out of it, the more remained behind. By 1815 his fertility had become almost uncanny, especially when we remember that he had for music only the leisure hours of a young schoolmaster of eighteen. In March he wrote the Mass in G; between March 25 and April 1 a string quartet in G-minor; in May a symphony (his third) in D-major; in June an entire operetta; during six days in July another operetta, of which the libretto fills forty-two closely printed pages; on October 15 seven songs; on the 19th four more; and in the interstices of time, another symphony, four other operettas, two piano sonatas, and one hundred and thirty-five songs, headed by "The Erl-King." One rubs one's eyes. Compared with Schubert's pen, Aladdin's lamp seems a poor affair.

The natural result, in worldly matters, of this imaginative preoccupation was abject poverty. Never did Apollo turn his back on Admetus with a more sublime indifference than in the avatar of this otherwise modest musician. It is true that he gave some scattering music lessons, and that for a time he acted as music-master in that same Esterhazy family which so long patronized Haydn; but of any lasting patronage, any remunerative appointment, or any systematic teaching, we hear nothing. Even his compositions brought him but a farcical revenue. He published nothing until 1821, when the first batch of songs, including "The Erl-King," was printed by subscription. Later, the publishers being still unwilling to take risks on a virtually unknown composer, twenty more songs were similarly issued. Only when popular favor had become manifest could he use the regular channels of publication; and then he had to content himself with the merest pittances. Diabelli, who in forty years is said to have gained over ten thousand dollars on "The Wanderer," paid Schubert for the plates and copyright of that and nineteen other songs only three hundred and fifty dollars. Haslinger, in the composer's last year, when his reputation was made and his work practically done, paid him one dollar and a quarter for half a dozen of his finest songs. That he was himself largely to blame for this pecuniary misfortune, through his aversion to drudgery and his carelessness in the conduct of business affairs, hardly reconciles us to the fact of his constant and often extreme poverty, but for which he might have lived longer and wrought to even better purpose.

But if he was poor, he had at least the temperament and tastes suitable to poverty. Not even Mozart, whose character and destiny had much in common with Schubert's, was more light-hearted and easy-going. "Perfect freedom of action," says his biographer, "was the element in which he by preference moved, and

for which he was content to make every sacrifice." To drink his mug of beer and eat his
sausage, to flirt with pretty servant-maids and
peasant girls, to discourse youthful philosophy
and play practical jokes with convivial poets,
painters, and students, above all to fill reams
of music paper with the melodies that were
always flooding his brain — this was his conception of sufficing happiness. It is curious to
read of his daily routine — how, rising early,
he would proceed, often before dressing, to im-
provise until breakfast; how, after a morning
spent in composition, he would dine at the
Gasthaus for a *Zwanziger* (ten cents); how he
would divide the rest of the day between walking in the suburbs, calling on the ladies of his
acquaintance, and discussing beer and friendship in Bogner's coffee-house, or the "Zur Un-
garischen Krone," or the "Zum rothen Kreuz,"
— sometimes, in these latter haunts, jotting
down immortal melodies on the backs of wine
cards in the midst of the tavern pandemonium. When he was in high spirits he would
challenge a friend to a mock duel with walk-
ing-sticks, or sing the "Erl-King," in parody,

through the teeth of a comb. And then there were the Schubertiaden, or Schubert evenings, held by his friends of both sexes in some one of the Vienna suburbs, at which the diversions consisted of dancing, *lieder*-singing, and theatricals, all to the accompaniment of the flowing bowl. "When the juice of the grape flowed in his veins," says one of his biographers, "he became a laughing tyrant, and would destroy everything he could, without making a noise, — glasses, plates, and cups, — and sit simpering and screwing up his eyes into the smallest possible compass." Altogether we get the picture of a Bohemian, irresponsible, bachelor life, innocent enough, but not troubled with embarrassing refinements. Schubert was not at his ease in highly cultivated circles. In his first letter from Zelész, the seat of the Esterhazys, he describes the servants in detail before giving a word to their princely employers. Physically Schubert was a short, stout man, with round shoulders, thick, blunt fingers, low forehead, projecting lips, stumpy nose, and short curly hair. Very near-sighted, he wore spectacles from boyhood. His friends' somewhat boorish wit compared him to a negro, a cabman, and even a tallow-candle, and afflicted him with the nickname of "Schwammerl," or "The Sponge" — whether in reference to his fondness for beer or to his superfluous flesh does not transpire.

The noteworthy fact toward which all these bits of otherwise insignificant personal detail point, the thesis in support of which they are here cited, is that Schubert was an unusually pure case of the sentimental temperament. All the external evidence — his contentedly ambling, unbuttoned existence, his combination of sweetness and a sort of involuntary nobility of aim, with an utter lack of intellectual distinction, his gullibility in business matters and practical affairs, his devotion to day-dream and revery, even his indolence and resulting sponginess of physique — points in the one direction. And these matters of ordinary observation are re-enforced by the internal evidence of his music, as for example the preference for short pieces, each vividly expressive of a single mood; the pervasive tone of tender sadness, frequently irradiated by charming fancy, but seldom swept aside by tumultuous passion and energy; the fondness for minor keys, delicious modulations, and persistent hypnotizing rhythms; the incapacity for complex structure and sustained imagination. Here, obviously, is no hero of abstract thought, like Bach, or of intellectual and emotional passion, like Beethoven, but a gracious sentimentalist, a man of feeling, a sort of Burns or Heine of music.

The natural medium of musical expression for such a temperament is the brief lyric, the song for single voice with piano accompaniment; and it was inevitable that Schubert, constituted as he was, should become "the father of the song." Before his time, this had been a form not favored by the great composers; Mozart's and Beethoven's songs, as Mr. Hadow has remarked, were merely the chips thrown off in a great workshop; for them the norm of expression was the symphony. But Schubert, as a new sort of man among composers, treated the song with a new kind of earnestness, and with an unprecedented spontaneity. Each of his best songs is an unsophisticated utterance of simple sentiment, a wondrously vivid presentment of a single isolated feeling, a "moment's monument," as Rossetti said the sonnet should be. And this was precisely what the artistic situation required. As in a short story of the kind that Kipling, Stevenson, and others have made familiar to us we do not demand that evolution of character, that complex nodation of plot, that subtle action and reaction of motive, which every great novel must have, but simply vividness, brilliant depiction of a single person, idea, or situation, so in a song we desire no symphonic grandeur of scope and wealth of ordered detail, but rather perfect utterance of a single highly specialized emotion.

Schubert's best songs fulfil this requirement in an almost inimitable degree. Simple in style and design, wonderfully direct and sincere, conceived as idealizations of the beautiful old German *Volkslieder*, and carried out with all the artistic perfection and appropriateness of detail that good craftsmanship could give, they are among the few things in music that are absolutely achieved. Especially remarkable is the art-concealing art by which Schubert, through some perfectly simple and unobtrusive feature of rhythm, melody, or harmony, knows how to suggest exactly the spirit and atmosphere of his text. In the well-known "Serenade," for example, the deftly managed mixture of minor and major harmonies (a favorite device, by the way, with Schubert) strikes just the right emotional note of loverly solicitude and tenderness. In "Am Meer" four chords at the beginning, and again at the end, bring the sombre, majestic ocean visibly before us, while the sudden dissonances introduced with the line "Fielen die Thränen nieder" bring home to us with a terrible poignancy the human tragedy which the poet has so vividly outlined against this stern natural background. And then turn to "Hark! Hark! the Lark," perhaps the most purely lovely, in a musical sense, of all the songs, and note the adorable elasticity of the rhythm, the lambent grace of the tune, the idyllic change of key at the words, "And winking Mary-buds begin to ope their golden eyes," and the poising flight of the melody at the final, "Arise — arise — arise": — truly Elizabethan this music, in its graciousness and childlike joy. In short, Schubert strikes at once, and in each case, in such songs as "Hark, hark! the Lark," "Who is Sylvia?" "Am Meer," "Du bist die Ruh," "Die Forelle," "Heidenröslein," and perhaps a dozen others, the exact tone and style needed to transfigure the particular feeling with all the magic of music, and throughout the song maintains the mood perfectly, with no mixture or clouding. And this, too, with the greatest actual diversity of mood in the different songs, to which his art flexibly responds. This group of his fifteen or twenty best songs is not only the crown of his own work, but one of the brightest jewels in the crown of romanticism.

In critical justice it is necessary to add, however, that in another group of his songs, even more popular than this supreme one, Schubert's romanticism inspired him less happily. Whenever, giving free rein to his passion for detailed expression, he directed his effort less towards reproducing an emotional mood than towards illustrating actual incidents, whenever, that is, he allowed dramatic rather than musical considerations to sway him, he produced a type of song which, in spite of its popularity, is intrinsically inferior, and hence likely to lose favor as musical taste develops. The most famous examples of this type are "The Erl-King" and "The Wanderer"; others scarcely less known are "Der Atlas," "Die Doppelgänger," "Die Junge Nonne," "Die Allmacht," "Kolma's Klage," and "Hagar's Klage." To hear the music of some of the songs of this class, unhappily large, after reading the commentaries of their admirers, is almost as cruel a disillusion as to eat the food at a cheap restaurant after a perusal of the pretentious and highly decorated bill of fare. Of "Die Allmacht," for example, Mr. A. B. Bach, in his book on "The Art Ballad," writes as follows: —

"This composition I would call a great tone-picture; it is a hymn of praise, stately and full of splendor. We seem to hear some prophet, who, with a voice of thunder, speaks to the people of the power and glory of the Almighty. The greatness of God in nature is first proclaimed. The tone-painting is full of grandeur and majesty. Not with the delicate, charming pencil of Fra Angelico, but with the strong, energetic, and powerful brush of Michael

Angelo, does Schubert paint the raging of the storm, the forest's boisterous violence, the thunder and the lightning. The painting is softer, milder, sweeter, only when he comes to the beautiful and calming words that the power of God is high above all, and greater when man feels it in his inmost heart. . . . Then follows a great crescendo, ending with the powerful and mighty exclamation, 'Great is Jehovah, the Lord!' which produces an overpowering effect. In this composition, as scarcely in any other, Schubert, usually so charming, is very dramatic, and shows command of the loftiest expression."

Turning, with expectation keyed high, from this rhapsody to the music of "Die Allmacht," what do we find? An annoyingly loud thumping of the piano, in its muddy lower register, for four pages on end, with no rhythmic relief; a vocal part more like a second-rate operatic recitative than one of those divine tunes of which Schubert had the secret; and to fill the cup of boredom, three rumbles of conventional musical "thunder," as threadbare and outworn as the antiquated theatrical properties described

by Steele in the "Tatler." It is hard to understand how any true lover of music can turn
from "Hark, hark! the Lark," or "Who is
Sylvia?" or "Du bist die Ruh," to such songs
as these, with their physically exciting tremolos,
crashing diminished-seventh chords, chromatic
climaxes, mysterious staccato octaves, pianissimo, in the bass, and other such claptrap effects,
better suited to accompany the drowning of the
heroine of melodrama than to edify the sense
of musical beauty. They reveal pitilessly the
seamy side of romanticism, and make us wish
that Schubert's fecund imagination had been
controlled by a more fastidious taste.

If the sentimentalist's tendency to value
emotion for itself, as the voluptuary wallows in
sensation, and the realist's fondness for crudely
detailed effect, sometimes led Schubert into an
artificial and fevered style, his very simplicity
at other times played him false. Simplicity in
art, as the case of Wordsworth has notoriously
proved, covers a wide range, from the sublime
to the ridiculous. Schubert is often sublimely
simple, as in "Du bist die Ruh," "Heidenröslein," "Der Leiermann"; but sometimes he

is merely flat and obvious. Indeed, writing, as he did, over six hundred songs in a score of years, not the most inspired of men could always have avoided platitude. Thus we must set aside many melodramatic and many trite compositions before we can get an unimpeded view of his real masterpieces. But after that has been done, we have left about twenty or thirty songs of such incomparable loveliness as to give him a secure place among the great masters of the musical lyric.

The careful discrimination between quantity and quality in Schubert's work, so obviously important in judging his songs, becomes perhaps even more indispensable when we come to his instrumental works. The facts that here present themselves to the intending student on his first approach to the subject are entirely misleading. Schubert wrote, he learns, ten symphonies and twenty string quartets, besides much other chamber and orchestral music. Remembering that Beethoven wrote nine symphonies and sixteen string quartets, he is likely to assume that the essential Schubert is to be found permeating the one set of works just as the essential Beethoven permeates the other, and that if he can take, so to speak, a critical average of them all, he will come at the true musical personality of their author. Nothing could be more erroneous. For it must be borne in mind that while the works of Beethoven were written during the entire period of his artistic maturity, from his twenty-fifth to his fifty-sixth year, and with the most laborious care, those of Schubert are largely youthful exercises, and were in many cases thrown off as one would write a letter. Schubert wrote voluminously and carelessly, and died at thirty-one, just as he was entering the prime of life. His works are thus, if one may say so, like his person, embedded in superfluous flesh. The bulk of them are, so far as representing him goes, pure surplusage, to be stripped off and thrown aside before we can see the outline and stature of his genius. The compositions produced before 1820 are interesting to-day only as documents bearing on the peculiar way in which his individual style was gradually developed. What they chiefly reveal is the ingenuousness, one might almost say the unconsciousness, with

which he habitually composed. He seems to
have made no effort to draw forth, by taking
thought, his shy and retiring individuality; his
method was rather to copy, often almost literally, the music he knew and liked, especially
that of Haydn and Mozart. The quartet in
G-minor, written in 1815, for example, contains
a perfectly Mozartish minuet, while its finale
is pure Haydn, except for occasional gleams
of Schubert in the happy exuberances of detail
and in the quick, informal modulations. Of
the symphony in B-flat, written in 1816, the
first and fourth movements are Haydn, the
second and third Mozart. The closeness of
the imitation is at times fairly disconcerting,
as in the last eight measures of the minuet,
which sound like a rejected sketch for the
minuet of the " Jupiter Symphony ":—

Figure I.

An even more amusing case is that of a passage in the E-major Quartet (opus 125, no. 2), written in the following year (1817), so startlingly like a portion of Mozart's G-minor Symphony that we can hardly resist the theory of unconscious plagiarism. The passages in question merit a careful comparison. If imitation is the sincerest flattery, Schubert was paying an eloquent tribute, indeed, to the genius of Haydn and Mozart in his works of 1815–1817.

Figure II.
SCHUBERT.

FRANZ SCHUBERT

cresc.

ff etc.

Mozart.

And
later:

83

Before 1818 there is little internal evidence that Schubert had felt at all the influence of the greatest musician of the period, Beethoven, with whom, if we may judge from his diary, he was not yet in complete sympathy. Under date of June, 1816, he compares disparagingly "that *bizarrerie* for which we have chiefly to thank one of the greatest German artists" with the "naturalness" and "purity" of the Italian, Salieri. In the C-major symphony of 1818, however, he has evidently fallen completely under the sway of the master. The first movement of this work shows a great advance over earlier symphonies; the orchestral resources are increased, and used with more skill; the themes are more concise and vigorous, more truly symphonic, though still showing a tendency to rhythmic monotony; the construction is ampler and more carefully planned, there being a slow introduction and a Beethovenish coda. The transition by which the repetition of the first section of the movement is approached shows afresh the curious literalness with which Schubert copied his models. The long poising, pianissimo, on a single harmony, and the final almost imperceptible lapse into the original key, are Beethoven to the letter. The other movements show the same

Figure III.

influence. Especially noteworthy are the substitution of a scherzo for the old-fashioned minuet, and, in the finale, the many sudden shifts of tonality by a semitone, and sudden alternations of extreme loud and soft. Here, as much as in the earlier things, it is true, Schubert remains the obedient and passive student; he is still, in the phrase of Stevenson, "playing the sedulous ape"; but his model is much more complex, his touch is surer, his technical facility greater, and he needs only to grow a little older, a little more mature and self-conscious, in order to stamp all these gradually acquired materials with his own individuality.

Now maturity comes to most men, the romanticists like the others, as a result of the suffering, misunderstanding, and disappointment that years have a way of bringing. The youth interprets all the world by his own freshness of enthusiasm, keen sensation, untrammelled imagination. Everything seems possible to him, and life is one long, romantic adventure. But when he actually comes in contact with that world which looked so fair from a distance, through the rosy glasses of temperament, he discovers that it is stubborn to his purposes, that it is full of alien wills with which he struggles in vain, and that this struggle reveals insurmountable weaknesses and limitations in himself. Then either bitterness, or a new understanding of himself, resignation to the inevitable, and interpretation of life in more universal terms, is bound to displace the old romantic egotism. Experience regroups itself in soberer colors, and if he be generous enough to escape cynicism he emerges from the ordeal chastened and humanized.

This transition from self-absorbed youth to magnanimous manhood came to Schubert between his twenty-third and twenty-seventh years, hastened by the adverse conditions of his life. We have seen how poverty held him in its sullen grasp; ill-health was added in 1824; and all through his last decade the sense of the indifference of the public to his higher artistic aims must have been dispiriting in the extreme. His songs were favorably enough received, but little interest was taken in his chamber and orchestral music except by a small circle of friends. That he could nevertheless go on, year after year, producing so splendid a series of compositions, in a spirit of such uncompromising devotion to art, almost entirely unsupported by public recognition, buoyed up by inward conviction alone, proves that underneath the careless Bohemianism of his everyday existence there was developing in him the stuff of real heroism. Like Columbus, he

> "found a world, and had no chart
> Save one that faith deciphered in the skies.
> To trust the soul's invincible surmise
> Was all his science and his only art."

The story of the last year of his short life is most pathetic. In March, 1828, he made an attempt to mend his fortunes by giving a concert of his own works, by which he earned one hundred and fifty dollars, to him a large sum. But no temporary help like this could count for much, so long as his compositions, the main business of his life, were so shamefully underrated by the publishers. For six of the best of the "Winterreise" songs he received a little over one dollar; for the E-flat Trio (opus 100), about four dollars and a half; for the great A-major Pianoforte Quintet (opus 114), a little over six dollars. His health being now seriously impaired, he wished to spend the summer in the country with friends, but was compelled by poverty to remain in the heat and confusion of Vienna. A momentary encouragement offered in a projected performance of his greatest work, the C-major Symphony, but it was given up as too difficult, and he never heard it. It was first performed eleven years after his death, by Mendelssohn, in Leipsic. In the fall he rapidly failed, and had just arranged to take lessons in counterpoint, with a view to yet greater works, when, after a comparatively short illness, he died, on November 19, 1828. He left no will, but from the official inventory of his effects we learn that he left behind him twenty-six dollars' worth of clothing and house furniture, and "a quantity of old music" (including the manuscript of the C-major Symphony), valued at five dollars.

Such were the dingy outer circumstances of this man's life. But his spirit soared above them. "My compositions," he wrote in his diary, "are the product of my mind, and spring from my sorrow; those only that were born of grief give the greatest delight to the outside world;" and in another place, more profoundly: "Certainly that happy joyous time is gone when every object seemed encircled with a halo of youthful glory; . . . and yet I am now much more than formerly in the way of finding peace and happiness in myself." But the best evidence we have that Schubert learned the lesson of sorrow, and not only transmuted bitter experience into immortal beauty but under the stress of that experience first found his true self, lies in the wonderful series of compositions which he wrote between 1820 and 1828. Here we find at last the essential Schubert. In the single movement in C-minor for string quartet, dated 1820, he discloses a new world of dramatic expression, earnest feeling, daring modulation, intricate harmony, and chromatic melody. And from this time on masterpiece followed masterpiece: the "Unfinished Symphony" in 1822; the A-minor Quartet and the Octet in 1824; the G-major and D-minor Quartets in 1826; the first two piano trios a year later; and to cap the climax, the C-major Quintet and the immortal C-major Symphony in 1828.

In spite of the emotional depth of these last works, the dominant note remains in them, as in everything that emanated from Schubert, romantic. Everywhere in them the interest of the romanticist in color for its own sake, in the primary sensuous charm of the tone combinations, is strikingly manifest. One of the hallmarks of Schubert's symphonies is his impressionistic treatment of orchestral tints, both pure and in mixture. None knows better than he how to make the oboe sultry or menacing, the clarinet mellow and liquid, the horn hollow, vague, mystical, the 'cellos passionate, and the violins clear, aspiring, and ethereal. The score of his C-major Symphony is a marvel of ingenuity and felicity in the weaving of various colors and modes of playing, as staccato and legato, pizzicato, etc. Look, for instance, at page 162 of Eulenberg's miniature score, and see how the wood-wind instruments chatter in staccato against the long rise and fall of the strings playing in octaves, legato; or at page 139, noting how, after a powerful climax and a moment of complete silence, the 'cello, against plucked chords by the other strings, sings a languorous melody, which is presently taken up by the oboe; or at pages 30–35, where, under the shimmering veil of the strings, the trombones gradually work out their sinister call, rising ever higher and higher, and finally precipitating all into the sounding turmoil of the climax on page 36. In such passages as these every tone sounds, and all unite harmoniously to produce the intended effect. In few scores will one find at once such richness and such clear transparency of coloring.

Nor is Schubert dependent for variety of color, as unimaginative composers are, on the richly diversified palette of the full orchestra. His chamber music shows how much he can accomplish with limited means. In his two trios, op. 99 and 100, by making the most of the percussion quality of the piano as well as of both the pizzicato and the sustained tones of the strings, he evolves a surprising variety from the three instruments. Even with the string quartet, the most monochromatic of chamber combinations, he achieves great differentiation and contrast, largely by rhythmically individualizing each voice. The opening of the

A-minor Quartet is a good example: viola and 'cello give a drone bass in a peculiar and striking rhythm (a dotted half-note followed by a group of four sixteenths); the second violin holds the tone-mass together by means of a graceful legato running figure in eighth-notes; the first violin sings a melody that follows its own free and untrammelled rhythm. One is reminded by such a passage of Dvořák, who is of close artistic kin to Schubert. Both men, in their writing for strings, secure fascinating texture by opposing many diverse rhythms simultaneously. The device has been assailed as being a mask to cover a poverty of real polyphony (inner melodiousness); but though it may to a certain extent be that, there can be no doubt of its sensuous effectiveness.

Another similarity between Schubert and Dvořák, also indicative of their romantic interest in special momentary features, is their coloristic use of harmony, and especially of modulation. Sudden transitions to remote keys are no commoner perhaps in Schubert than in Beethoven, but in Schubert they are prompted by considerations of color rather than of design.

Like Dvořák, he loves unexpected recrystalliza-
tions of tone. He shakes the kaleidoscope of
his fancy, and all the bits of glass fall into a
new pattern (tonality). Such a fascinating
change as that immediately after the *forte* chord
of D, in the second entr'acte of "Rosamunde,"
is an illustration. Even better ones, because
showing so clearly the lack of any element of
formal design in these changes, are those casual
alternations of major and minor mode which
are so frequent as to constitute a mannerism.
At the close of the first movement of the G-
major Quartet is an extreme case. Four
measures consist entirely of abrupt alternations
of the major and minor tonic chords, with no
melodic binding together. This is obviously
purely a color effect, and its motive is of course
unequivocally romantic.

Romantic also is the persistent lyricism of all
Schubert's music, the symphonies and quartets
as well as the songs and piano pieces. In the
larger almost as much as in the smaller works,
the fundamental trait of the peculiar type of
expression used is its subjectivity, its strong
personal flavor. If the songs of the classicists

seem often like condensed symphonies, the symphonies of this romanticist are in many respects magnified songs. In several of his instrumental movements Schubert actually transcribes his themes from songs already written, as for example in the variations of the D-minor Quartet, founded on "Death and the Maiden," and those of the "Forellen Quintet," founded on "Die Forelle." When he uses entirely new material, he is apt to conceive it in the lyrical style, and even to cast it in the lyrical form, with an exact balance of phrases of equal length. The second subject in the "Unfinished Symphony," for instance, is like a stanza or strophe; the imagination easily adds words to it; it is an instrumental song. Most of Schubert's more emotional themes share this quality of utterances, and seem rather communications of personal feeling than objects of abstract beauty. Even in the later works, like the D-minor and G-major Quartets and the C-major Quintet, in which the romance is tinged with tragedy, it is still, one feels, romantic tragedy, the tragedy of sentiment and sensibility, and not universal cosmic tragedy like Beethoven's or Bach's.

Yet there is in these later works, also, an intensity and breathlessness of utterance, a white heat of passion burning away all dross and surplusage, and giving the style an incisiveness strongly contrasted with Schubert's usual genial prolixity, which seem to emanate from some sterner, wilder element in his nature. There is a nervous tenseness here which is distinctively modern; the D-minor Quartet particularly has the modern closeness of texture and rapidity of pulse. Its first theme, unlike most of Schubert's, is a short and trenchant motive of five notes, compelling attention from the very outset. The entire first movement is treated with great depth of feeling and sustained power, and the coda is of a wonderful dignity and reticence. The final presto, too, reminds us of Schumann in its emotional richness, and of Tschaïkowsky in the passion of its broken rhythms and headlong harmonic progressions. On the other hand, the harmonic idiom of the first movement of the quartet in G-major (see Figure IV.), with its lapses of triads down through intervals of a whole step, is that of César Franck. Schubert is here the

prototype of the most advanced modern symphonists, as in his piano pieces he anticipates
the methods of Schumann, Chopin, and Liszt,
and in his songs gives the cue to Franz, Rubin-
stein, Grieg, and Brahms.

Figure IV.

The chief faults of Schubert's instrumental
works — and they are grave ones — result in
part from his way of composing, and in part
from the untraversable opposition between
the lyrical expression native to him and the
modes of construction suitable to extended
movements. Schubert was an easy-going, careless, and indolent writer. He wrote music as
most people write letters; often he would
scribble off half a dozen songs in a single day;
he thought nothing of making an overture in
three hours, or a whole operetta in a week;
to a friend who asked him how he composed,
he replied, "As soon as I finish one thing I begin
another." What all this means, practically, is
that he did not "compose" at all in the strict
sense of placing together tones with care and

forethought, but merely improvised on paper.
And as a result, while he certainly attained a
delightful spontaneity of effect, he also fell into
the pitfalls of monotony and diffuseness. He
is constantly becoming hypnotized by a rhythm,
keeping it up relentlessly, page on page, without relief. When he has once hit upon a phrase
that appeals to him, such, for example, as the
second subject in the G-major Quartet, he is
apt to adhere to it pretty closely through a
whole section of the piece. Such insistence,
in contrast to the variety of phraseology of
composers like Mozart, is comparable in effect
to the singsong couplets of Pope or Dryden, as
contrasted with the pliant versification of
Shelley. This weaker aspect of Schubert, connected with his lack of intellectual vigor and
possibly with a certain flabbiness of moral
fibre, has been exhaustively discussed by Mr.
H. H. Statham, an English critic, who reaches
the conclusion that "in music, as in literature,
easy writing is hard reading," and that in Schubert's larger pieces "lovely melodies follow each
other, but nothing comes of them." Whether
or not we agree with so extreme a view, we

cannot deny Schubert's weakness in musical construction.

We usually find in his music five pages of repetition to one of real development. Mr. Statham is right in contrasting the "vain repetitions" in the andante of the C-major Symphony with the logical evolution of matter in the allegretto of Beethoven's Seventh Symphony. And even where, as in the fine coda of the finale of the C-major Symphony, Schubert has a truly broad design to work out, he fills in his detail in the easiest, least exacting way by repeating identical phrases at a higher and higher pitch. The effect of the long, gradual climax is intensely dramatic, but when upon familiarity we realize that the ideas generate, so to speak, by fission, or exact reduplication, rather than by organic evolution, we are left æsthetically unsatisfied. The truth seems to be that Schubert, being essentially a lyrical writer, makes beautiful symphonies and quartets in spite of, rather than by means of, the natural conditions of these epic musical forms. His symphonies are expanded songs, delightful, as songs are delightful, for their directness of feeling, their beauty of detail, their warmth of color and sensuous charm.

His last work, however, the great C-major Symphony, has enough of the heroic about it to make us cautious in saying what he might or might not have done had he not died at thirty-one, when he was just entering the period of artistic maturity. There is a grandeur of scale and intention, a deliberation and solidity, a sustained power, large touch, and freedom of execution about this symphony that place it above all his other works. The long climaxes bespeak a reserve power not associated with Schubert the song-writer; the themes wear their possibilities less upon the surface, and unfold them more cumulatively; the harmony is firmer, plainer, and stronger; the scoring is done as it were with a larger brush, the colors laid on in wider spaces and freer patterns; and in the last movement the romantic note is for once well drowned in a deeper cry of tragic heroism. It is not a mere coincidence that the theme at the beginning of the development section so strongly suggests Beethoven's "Hymn of Joy"; the spirit here is Beethoven's, and the spaciousness of the scheme of construction, if not the detail with which it is filled in, are worthy of the greatest symphonist. Here surely the graciousness of childhood and the romantic dalliance of youth are laid aside, and Schubert speaks with the deep, deliberate voice of manhood. Death never came to an artist more untimely. Had he lived, we cannot tell what new and even profounder expressions of the ripe earnestness that lies beyond romance he might not have planned and achieved.

III
ROBERT SCHUMANN

—

ROBERT SCHUMANN
From a painting by E. Bendemann

III

ROBERT SCHUMANN

—

❧

IN the year 1830, in the old German university town of Heidelberg, Robert Schumann, then a youth of twenty, a reluctant student of law, and a devoted lover of music, was making the most momentous decision of his life. For us, to whom his music is a *fait accompli*, it is easy enough to see the way his genius pointed; for him it was a time of self-searching, of beckoning hopes and haunting fears, of long hesitation before the final courageous adventure into an unknown land. "My whole life," he writes his mother, "has been a twenty years' struggle between poetry and prose, or, if you like to call it so, Music and Law. Now I am standing at the crossroads, and am scared at the question 'Which way to choose.'" "Let me draw a parallel," he continues. "*Art* says: 'If you are industrious, you may reach the goal in three years.' *Juris-prudence* says: 'In three years you may perhaps be an "Accessist," earning sixteen *groschen* a year.' *Art* continues: 'I am as free as air; the whole world is open to me.' *Jurisprudence* shrugs her shoulders, and says: 'I am nothing but red tape, from the clerk to the judge, and always go about spick-and-span, and hat in hand.' *Art* goes on to say: 'Beauty and I dwell together, and my whole world and all my creations are in the heart of man. I am infinite and untrammelled, and my works are immortal.' *Jurisprudence* says, with a frown: 'I can offer you nothing but bumpkins and lawsuits, or at the utmost a murder, but that is an unusual excitement. I cannot edit new Pandects.' My beloved mother, I can but faintly indicate the thoughts which are surging through my brain. I wish you were with me now, and could look into my heart. You would say: 'Start on your new career with courage, industry, and confidence, and you cannot fail.'" [1]

Certainly there was little enough in the legal

---

[1] "Early Letters of Robert Schumann," trans. by M. Herbert, London, 1888, pp. 113, 118.

profession to attract a youth such as these early letters reveal, ardent, imaginative, romantically intolerant of the humdrum and the prosaic. From the first we see him, in this clear mirror of his own words, marked for a life of artistic expression and free creation. He has all the artist's susceptibility to impressions, both sensuous and intellectual, as we gather from his rhapsodies over the landscapes, peasant maidens, and wines of the Rhine Valley, and from his interest in the individualities of his travelling companions. He is a creature of moods, plunged in a day from heights of joy into abysses of melancholy. He is impetuous, generous, and volatile in his boyish friendships and love affairs; an affectionate but inconsiderate son, an ardent but desultory worker, a voluminous but irregular correspondent, irresponsible in money matters, impatient of social usages, inconstant in almost everything but his devotion to beauty. The idol of his boyish hero worship is Jean Paul Richter, that curiously German compound of sentimentality, mysticism, and wayward humor; he wishes that all mankind might read Richter and become "better and more unhappy;" and he often favors his mother with Jean-Paulish apothegms, reflections, and fantasies, in which platitude and sincerity are mixed as only enthusiastic boyhood can mix them. Byron, Heine, and the other romantic poets of the day he reads, too, with avidity, and imitates them in erotic ballads and plays about picturesque robbers. And all along, music is the language of his deepest moods, and he spends hours communing with his piano in rhapsodic improvisation, and devotes his leisure to composing musical character-sketches of his friends.

By such a youth the choice between law and music could hardly be decided but in one way. He persuaded his mother and his guardian to allow him six months in Leipsic, under the teaching of Friedrich Wieck, to show what he could make of himself as a pianist. His letters during this period of the first steady labor he had known, when the reaction necessarily following the feverish weeks of decision plunged him into a dull and relaxed state, show the sterling side of his meteoric nature. They complete the picture of one of the most lovable of youths. "I just keep jogging on," he writes in May, 1831. "It is the fault of all vivid young minds that they aspire to too much at once; it only makes their work more complicated, and their spirit more restless. . . . If only I could do one thing well, instead of many things badly, as I have always done! Still, the principal thing for me to keep in mind is to lead a pure, steady, sober life. If I stick to that, my guardian angel will not desert me; he now sometimes almost possesses me for a little." A few months later he continues, more tranquilly: "If one has at last come to a conclusion, and is quiet and satisfied in one's own mind, the ideas of honor, glory, and immortality, of which one dreams, without doing anything toward their accomplishment, all resolve themselves into gentle rules, only to be learned from time, life, and experience. To bring to light anything great and calmly beautiful, one ought only to rob Time of one grain of sand at a time; the complete whole does not appear all at once, still less does it drop from the sky. It is only natural that there should be moments when we think we are going back, while in reality we are only hesitating in going on. If we let such moments pass, and then set to work again quickly and bravely, we shall get on all right."

The philosophic calm thus gained by habits of regular work was soon to be sorely taxed; for in that very year all Schumann's hopes of ever becoming a piano virtuoso were shattered by an accident to his right hand. With characteristic impatience he had devised a mechanism for hastening the independence of the refractory fourth finger by holding it up with a string while the others practised. Of course the result of this violence was a permanent lameness. Under this affliction, however, was hidden an incidental benefit; for piano playing became now no longer one of the many things that he did badly, as he had complained, and he had at last all his attention to concentrate upon composition. He had written his opus 1, "Variations on the name of Abegg," in 1830; he now followed this up with an endless stream of charming piano pieces, the like of which had never before been seen. In 1830–31 came the "Papillons," opus 2, and the "Allegro," opus 8; in 1832 the "Studies after Paganini" (in which the technical interest of the virtuoso is still paramount), the "Intermezzi," and the fascinating "Impromptus on a Theme of Clara Wieck"; 1833 added to the list two more primarily technical works, the "Concert Études on Caprices of Paganini" and the splendid "Toccata," opus 7; and in the next six years, up to 1839, came a long series of unique and lovely things, among which stand forth in especial prominence those romantic whimsicalities, the "Davidsbündlertänze," the "Carnaval," and "Kriesleriana," the somewhat less successful, because more ambitious, Sonatas, opuses 11, 14, and 22, and the more mature "Symphonic Études," "Kinderscenen," "Phantasie," and "Novelettes."

These piano works, conceived with most daring originality and executed with inimitable verve, deserve to take rank with Schubert's songs, Mendelssohn's overtures, and Chopin's nocturnes and preludes, among the very few supreme and perfect attainments of the romantic spirit in music. Their exuberant vitality, their prodigal wealth of melodic invention, their rhythmic vigor and harmonic luxuriance, their absolutely novel pianistic effects, their curious undercurrent of fanciful imagery and extra-musical allusion, the peculiarly personal, even perverse, idiom in which they are couched, all conspire to make them unique even among their author's works, and in some respects more happily representative of him than the later productions in which he was more in-fluenced by conventional or borrowed ideals. In them we have the wild-flavored first fruits of his genius, fresh with all the aroma and bloom of unsophisticated youth.

A curious feature of most of these early pieces, due to the literary cultivation and to the fanciful bias of their composer's mind, is their constant reference to all sorts of extra-musical interests. Schumann, at this time almost as much a man of letters as of tones, took pleasure in equipping his pieces with an ingenious and amusing series of allusions to places and people, real and fictitious, a kind of running commentary of footnotes on the music, comprehensible only to the initiated. This is managed partly by means of spelling out words in the letters which stand for musical tones,[1] partly by directions printed above the music, like stage directions in a play, and partly by mottoes, both musical and literary, and quotations of original and other melodies. The "Variations," opus 1, are founded on a theme which spells A-B-E-G-G — a pseudonym given by Schumann to a lady whose beauty he had admired.

Figure V.

Most of the pieces in the "Carnaval" are founded on four tones spelling A-S-C-H, in honor of a friend who lived in the town of that name, the rhythms being so ingeniously varied that each theme sounds new in spite of its set tonal basis.

Figure VI.   "PIERROT."

A   Es   C   H

[1] In German the terminology of letters standing for tones is richer than in English. B is our B-flat, while H stands for our B-natural; Es is E-flat; As, A-flat, etc.

In later life Schumann wrote six organ fugues on the name B-A-C-H; in the album of Gade, the Danish composer, he wrote a theme spelling "G-A-D-E, A-D-E" ("Gade, farewell"); and the "Northern Song," in his "Piano Pieces for the Young," is founded on the same letters, in honor of the same musician.

Mottoes and quotations meet us at every turn. Printed above one of the melodies in the "Intermezzi" are the words "Meine Ruh' ist hin" — "My peace is gone." The "Davidsbündlertänze" bear at their head a stanza of verses, and commence with a musical motto by Clara Wieck. In the final march of the "Carnaval," a melody of the seventeenth cen-

tury, "The Grandfather's Dance," is used to
symbolize the futile resistance of pedantic conservatism to the progress of art. The "Phantasie," opus 17, was to have been called "Obo-
los," the purpose of its composition being to
contribute to a fund for a monument of Beethoven, and the separate movements were to
have received the highly fanciful titles, "Ruins,"
"Triumphal Arch," and "The Starry Crown";
but Schumann finally contented himself with a
motto from Schlegel: —

> "*Durch alle Töne Tönet*
> *Im bunten Erdentraum*
> *Ein leiser Ton gezogen*
> *Für den der heimlich lauschet.*" [1]

In the "Faschingsschwank aus Wien" (Carni-
val Prank at Vienna) he manages the musical
quotation with felicitous humor. It seems
that the playing of the "Marseillaise" was at that
time forbidden by the German authorities, on
account of the strongly revolutionary tendencies
of public feeling. This police taboo did not
prevent Schumann from letting a single strain
of the splendid tune flash out from his mosaic

[1] See page 128 for Schumann's comment on this motto.

of melodies, to the unbounded delight of his audience and the discomfiture of the helpless officials.

Of all his compositions, the "Davidsbündler-tänze" is fullest of this tricksy play of imagination, in which he took, as Oscar Bie says, "the pleasure of the delicate man of taste in labelling." From about 1834, when he founded his musical journal, the *Neue Zeitschrift für Musik*, the imaginary society of the *Davidsbund* played an important part in his mental life. Believing that it was a part of his duty to oppose the philistinism, the dulness, pedantry, and sensuality which pervaded the music of the day, he dramatized the conflict as a struggle between the *Davidsbund*, or club of Davidites, and the forces of Philistia. His fancy played about this central conception until it had evolved a whole company of Davidites, individualizing each one. Several were merely single aspects of their creator's complex temperament. Florestan was the impassioned Schumann, Eusebius the dreamy and tender Schumann, Raro the philosophical mediator between the two. Others indicated friends: Felix Meritis was Mendelssohn; Chiarina, Clara Wieck; Estrella, Ernestine von Fricken, an early sweetheart. Once projected into the actual world, these figments of fancy became very real to their creator. His Sonata, opus 11, was originally printed as "by Florestan and Eusebius." Each of the numbers of the "Davidsbündlertänze" is signed "F.," or "E.," or "F. and E.," and the ascription is always conscientiously justified by the character of the music. In the first edition there are even "stage directions," such as, "Here Florestan stops, his lips trembling painfully," and "Eusebius said too much about this; but his eyes were full of joy." These finical particularities, however, as well as the motto in verse, were in the second edition stricken out.

All these elaborate paraphernalia with which Schumann equipped his first essays in composition are noteworthy not so much for any intrinsic significance as for the light they throw on his peculiar attitude toward an art which most of his predecessors had approached in a wholly objective and detached spirit. The persistent and minute subjectivity they reveal is remarkable in so young a man, working by instinct and in despite of the powerful influence of tradition. Most men approach music through a systematic technical discipline, and achieve individuality of style only with maturity; Schumann, reversing the process, turns to music at first simply as to one of several available ways of expressing a lively imagination, and gains technical skill but gradually and by arduous effort. His eloquence is that of a man filled with matter and enthusiasm, but untrained in oratory; he stammers, hesitates, coins words, improvises phraseology as he goes, and in the end attains fluency by dint of sheer earnestness and conviction. The inner impulse to expression creates its own medium, instead of being itself formed by the medium available; and while a language thus derived offhand has necessarily certain crudities, it has also, of course, a delightful freshness and happy spontaneity.

The inexhaustible tunefulness of the early Schumann is little short of marvellous. Few composers have been so prodigal of lovely melodies. They are like the king's daughters in the fairy tales, each more beautiful than the last; and though there is doubtless a family resemblance, each has a distinct physiognomy, a pronounced individuality. They are, for the most part, indeed, brief, striking motives rather than deliberately composed tunes, perfect but minute crystals of most various shapes, forming spontaneously in the highly saturated solution of the musical thought. No effort is made to purify, separate, or collect them; what their composer seems chiefly to value is their profusion and luxuriance. To state the same thing in more technical terms, there is next to no thematic development; there is simply the presentation of one charming phrase after another. The result is of course a certain fragmentariness and whimsicality; the music impresses us not by its cumulative power, its orderly advance, but by the sheer charm of its primitive elements.

The vigor of the rhythms never flags. Short notes in "dotted rhythms," holds from unaccented to accented beats, and all manner of devices for intensifying accentuation, give an inimitable elasticity to such things as the first of the "Intermezzi," the sixth, seventh, ninth, and final sections of the "Impromptus on a Theme of Clara Wieck," the ninth of the "Davidsbündlertänze," "Préambule," "Coquette," "Chiarina," "Valse Allemande," and the final march in the "Carnaval," "Aufschwung" in the "Phantasiestücke," and many others. There is to be observed also a constant tendency to emphasize the metre by slight but systematic deviations from it, such as syncopation and the shifting of motives into artificial relations to the measure, and the simultaneous use of two or more metrical schemes at once. Interesting examples of this sort of intensive syncopation occur in "Grillen," one of the "Phantasiestücke," in the B-flat major section of the eighth "Novelette," and in the "Faschingsschwank aus Wien." A delightfully quaint use of shifted motives is made in the finale of the Sonata, opus 11. The theme of the movement, though written in triple measure, consists entirely of two-beat motives, so that there is a constantly felt, and very exciting, opposition between metrical and rhetorical accents.

Figure VII.
Measure accent.
Motive accent.

The motive of the scherzo of the same work is treated in a somewhat similar way. Of all the many instances which might be mentioned of a simultaneous use of two metrical schemes, one of the most consummate is the employment, in "Des Abends," of three groups of two sixteenth-notes in the melody, against two groups of three sixteenths in the accompaniment — a subtlety often missed by pianists, but essential to the charm of the piece. The first two numbers of the "Davidsbündlertänze" also present attractive oppositions of metre.

The same waywardness finds further expression in certain harmonic eccentricities. Schumann loves to surprise, waylay, disappoint, and otherwise cajole his hearer. Strong unprepared dissonances, entrances of chords before we expect them, delays of the expected ones, entire evasions of the seemingly inevitable, and felicitous transitions into the seemingly impossible are a constant feature of his program.

He loves to hit upon a note as if by accident, and then to justify and even emphasize it, as in the eighth and succeeding measures of the theme of the "Papillons"; to wound our ears with the harshest intervals, and then compel our acquiescence by a resulting felicity, as in the introduction to the F-sharp minor Sonata; to toss us restlessly upon a chromatic sea and bring us out at last into diatonic tranquillity, as in the first two pages of the "Toccata." At the beginning of the "Kreisleriana" he keeps the right hand half a pace ahead of the left, thus producing a great richness of tone as well as emphasizing the vigorous progression of the bass. In the first variation in opus 5 just the reverse of this occurs; the bass takes the lead, while the chords in the right hand lag behind, making temporary discords, but always coming out right in the end.

Many of these peculiarities of harmony are doubtless due simply to Schumann's sensuous susceptibility to good ear-filling sound, long intensified and developed by his habit of improvisation. Sir Hubert Parry remarks that "he loved to use all the pedal that was possible, and had but little objection to hearing all the notes of the scale sounding at once. He is said to have liked dreaming to himself, by rambling through all sorts of harmonies with the pedal down; and the glamour of crossing rhythms and the sound of clashing and antagonistic notes was most thoroughly adapted to his nature." There is, indeed, evidence of this taste for rich tonal effects on almost every page of his piano music. Like Chopin he finds a Mozartian clarity of sound a little tame, and prefers to obscure the outlines of his consonant chords by means of plentifully sprinkled dissonances; but while Chopin, more fastidiously delicate, makes his dissonances float like a diaphanous veil over the pure chords, Schumann, with true Teutonic luxuriousness, fills up all the chinks and crannies with suspensions and passing notes, and holds down the pedal to boot. His piano style is much more massive than Chopin's. He has the true Johnsonian taste for sonorousness and resonance. His ear is insatiably curious, too; witness the final chord in the "Papillons," with its tones released successively until but one remains sounding, the extraordinary clangor of low thirds and final emergence of ghostly pianissimo chord at the end of "Paganini" in the "Carnaval," and the many bizarre sonorities he obtains by making the left hand play above the right, as in the second of the "Abegg Variations" and in the section marked "Langsamer" in number two of the "Kreisleriana."

Taken all together, these piano compositions of the decade 1830–1840, which may be called the first period of Schumann's artistic life, reveal an extraordinarily mobile and fanciful temperament, working with the greatest freedom and spontaneity, though without the guidance of regular discipline. Their crudities are undeniable: the flights are short, the forms are fragmentary and often badly proportioned, the style is highly subjective, eccentric, arbitrary. Yet there is in these things such unflagging vitality, such rare and various beauty, such abounding youthful enthusiasm and freshness, that one would hardly sacrifice them for anything else that music has to offer, and it has even been questioned whether in the final analysis there is not more of the true Schumann in them than in the later, larger, and more technically perfect works. In a sense Hans von Bülow was right in saying that the *ipsissimus* Schumann was to be found only in the early works up to opus 50.

However this may be, it is certain that at about his thirtieth year Schumann's artistic ideal began to undergo a gradual but radical transformation. We see him in the compositions of this time paying less and less attention to those purely personal whims and fancies that had at first dominated his imagination, and beginning to work very earnestly toward objective beauty and impersonal expression. The fictitious characters, the mottoes, the stage directions, the whole elaborate machinery of allusion to extra-musical interests, are forgotten, and the interest of the music itself becomes all in all. There had been already, among the works of his "storm and stress period," single compositions in which the dramatic interest was wholly subordinated to the musical, as, for example, the great "Toccata," opus 7, the "Allegro," opus 8, and the "Novelettes," opus 21; but now what had been only occasional in the days when fancy and a self-involved emotional life absorbed him grew to be normal and constant, and he became for the first time a liberal and devoted artist. Of the causes underlying this important change, the most fundamental was doubtless simply increasing maturity. Youth is naturally and innocently egotistical; the young man of sensibility loses himself in day dreams and whimsical fancies, which have no basis in experience, and no reference to anything beyond themselves; age brings a sense of the values of real life, sobers and domesticates the passions, and enlarges the interests until they spread from the self to all humanity. In an artistic nature this general change of attitude involves a change of artistic ideal; poignancy, intensity of expression, become less valued than justice and proportion; the merely self-expressive comes to seem trivial, and whimsicalities are discarded as interfering with the serenity of a universal beauty. Schumann's change of attitude was simply an unusually striking case of what happens to every perceptive mind when experience has been sufficiently assimilated.

The anxieties, doubts, fears, and disappointments connected with his courtship of Clara Wieck probably did more than anything else to chasten and to steady his character at this time.[1] The two artists, so diverse in talents, so remarkably at one in musical ideals, had first met in Leipsic in 1828, when one was a law student and amateur musician of eighteen, and the other an accomplished pianist, though only nine years old. Their relation was for a while purely musical; but as Clara's mind gradually developed, and especially after she began to play Schumann's compositions, they discerned more and more how deep-seated an artistic and personal congeniality was destined to bind them together. It is most interesting to trace in his letters and published music the successive steps of their comradeship. In 1832 he composes his "Impromptus on a Theme of Clara Wieck"; in 1833 he writes: "I have had a sympathetic idea, namely that

[1] The remarkable story of this courtship is told at length in "Clara Schumann, Ein Künstlerleben," by Berthold Litzmann, Zweiter Band, Leipsic, 1906. It has also been vividly sketched in English by Mr. Richard Aldrich, in an article in *Music*, vol. 18.

to-morrow, exactly at eleven o'clock, I shall play the Adagio from Chopin's 'Variations,' and shall think intensely, exclusively, of you. My petition is that you will do the same, so that we may meet and communicate in spirit;" in 1834 he says: "When I am thinking of you very intently I invariably find myself at the piano, and seem to prefer writing to you in chords of the ninth, and especially with the familiar chord of the thirteenth." "Chiarina," in the "Carnaval," written in 1835 and 1837, is a musical portrait of the already beloved Clara, and the F-sharp minor Sonata, dating from the same period, one of his most romantic and impassioned works, is dedicated to her. The "Davidsbündlertänze" (1837) opens with a motive by her, and in 1839, while he is busy with the "Phantasie," he tells her, "I suppose you are the *Ton* in the motto." As time goes on, musical sympathy merges more and more into love. "The 'Davidsbündlertänze,' and 'Phantasiestücke,'" he writes in January, 1838, "will be finished in another week. There are many bridal thoughts in the dances, which were suggested by the most delicious excitement that I ever remember. My Clara will understand all that is contained in the dances, for they are dedicated to her more emphatically than any of my other things. The whole story is a Polterabend."[1] In April he observes ingenuously, "I have just noticed that Ehe[2] [the German for "marriage"] is a very musical word, and a fifth, too." A year later he exclaims: "From your Romance I see plainly that we are to be man and wife. Every one of your thoughts comes out of my soul, just as I owe all my music to you. . . . Once I can call you mine you shall hear plenty of new things. . . . And we will publish some things under *our two names*, so that posterity may regard us as one heart and one soul, and may not know which is yours and which mine. How happy I am!"

Meanwhile, however, the narrow selfishness of the father, Friedrich Wieck, was raising all sorts of obstacles to this union. His daughter being, by her playing in public, a source of

---

[1] Eve of a wedding day.

[2] H, it will be remembered, stands in German for the note B-natural, which makes the musical interval of a fifth with E.

financial gain to him, he steadily opposed a marriage, as unfavorable to his interests. He forbade the lovers to meet, circulated false and damaging stories of Schumann, and when the couple, goaded to despair by his insensate obstinacy, had resolved to take matters into their own hands, thwarted even so radical a step by pretending to yield, but imposing conditions that could not possibly be carried out. On the whole, considering his impulsive temperament, Schumann bore this persecution with admirable patience, though not without an occasional plaint. "Your father calls me phlegmatic? 'Carnaval' and phlegmatic! F-sharp minor Sonata and phlegmatic! Being in love with such a girl and phlegmatic! And you can listen calmly to all this? He says that I have written nothing in the *Journal* for six weeks. In the first place, it is not true; secondly, even if it were, how does he know what other work I have been doing? Up to the present the *Journal* has had about eighty sheets of my own ideas, not counting the rest of my editorial work, besides which, I have finished ten great compositions in two years, and they have cost me some heart's blood. To add to all this, I have given several hours' hard study every day to Bach and Beethoven, and to my own work, and conscientiously managed a large correspondence. I am a young man of twenty-eight, with a very active mind, and an artist to boot; yet for eight years I have not been out of Saxony, and have been sitting still, saving my money, without a thought of spending it on amusement or horses, and quietly going my own way, as usual. And do you mean to say that all my industry and simplicity, and all that I have done, is quite lost upon your father?"

But all these difficulties and disappointments, all these occasions for patience, tact, industry, loyalty, and self-control, painful as they were to experience, were slowly transforming the capricious and dreamy youth into a man of mature will and seasoned resourcefulness. "No man is any use," says Stevenson, "until he has dared everything." Some such conviction must have been in Schumann's mind when at last, early in 1840, he resolved to avail himself of the law of Saxony that when parents withhold their consent to a marriage without good reason, the consent of the courts may be substituted. For such a man, so public a step in so sacredly private a matter must have been doubly difficult; to decide upon it must have involved a long mental turmoil. But he did finally take his case to the courts, and eventually married Clara Wieck, with the sanction of the law, in September, 1840. With this manly and courageous action his youth may be said to have ended, and the responsibilities, anxieties, labors, and sober joys of his manhood to have commenced.

It thus happens that the last purely lyrical expression of his essentially lyrical genius is to be found in the fine series of songs which he poured forth in 1840. In the early months of this, his "song-year," he was in a most sensitive and exalted state. The prospect of attaining the goal so long vainly striven for had fired his imagination to fever heat; and according to his habit he relieved this excitement by incessant composition. "Since yesterday morning," he writes in February, "I have written about twenty-seven pages of music (something new), and I can tell you nothing more about it, except that I laughed and cried over it with delight. Ah, Clara, what bliss it is writing for the voice, and I have had to do without it for so long!" This "something new" was the cycle of "Myrthen" songs, opus 25, among which are "Widmung," "Der Nussbaum," "Die Lotosblume," "Du Bist wie eine Blume," and others almost equally earnest, tender, and passionate. With his first published songs (nine lyrics by Heine, opus 24) he sends the message: "Here is a slight reward for your last two letters. While I was composing these songs I was quite lost in thoughts of you. If I were not engaged to such a girl, I could not write such music." "I have been composing so much," he writes in May, "that it really seems quite uncanny at times. I cannot help it, and should like to sing myself to death, like a nightingale. There are twelve songs of Eichendorff's [the 'Liederkreis,' opus 39, containing the dramatic 'Waldesgespräch,' the ethereal 'Mondnacht,' and the splendidly passionate 'Frühlingsnacht'], but I have nearly forgotten them, and begun something else."

All together, over one hundred songs were produced during this single year, including such immortal masterpieces as "Er, der Herrlichste von Allen," "Im wunderschönen Monat Mai," "Ich grolle nicht," "Ich hab' im Traum geweinet," and "Die Beiden Grenadiere," in addition to those already mentioned. In general, the songs have the same melodic freshness, richness of harmony, color, vigor of rhythm, and individuality of style that distinguish the earlier piano works. It is noteworthy, however, that in a certain directness of utterance, in freedom from eccentricities of manner and perversity of fancy, and in an increased breadth and coherence of structure, they show a distinct advance. They mark, indeed, a point of transition in Schumann's career, a point at which, still retaining the exuberance of youth, he has just learned to direct and control it by means of a more efficient artistry, and in the service of a maturer ideal. To most of his other works a strict criticism has reluctantly to admit the pertinence, on one side or the other, of the proverb "*Si jeunesse savait, si vieilesse pouvait*";

but the songs seem as thoroughly achieved as they are richly inspired.

After his marriage he turned to the larger forms of composition, which he took up in a curiously methodical rotation. First came, in 1841, three symphonies, the B-flat major, opus 38, the so-called "Overture, Scherzo, and Finale," and the D-minor, published many years later as opus 120. The piano concerto was also begun. In 1842 his interest was shifted to chamber music, and the three quartets for strings, the piano quartet, and the piano quintet appeared in rapid succession. Not until 1843 did he essay, in "Paradise and the Peri," a large choral work, but thereafter several such works appeared from time to time. Thus we see that while his more romantic compositions were for the most part produced in the years of youth and courtship, he turned, when once he had begun to face life as it is, in all its tragedy and difficulty as well as its human beauty and sweetness, to the severer, grander forms of music. In spite of the happiness he found in one of the most perfect of marriages, we must remember that this union also involved new responsibilities, anxieties, and distractions. It brought with it novel social and professional duties, children to be protected, guided, and helped, and above all the grinding routine by which the daily bread of an artist has to be earned. How severe the conditions were we have only recently learned from the complete biography of Clara Schumann.[1] In her diary we read of the constant struggles of these sensitive people to get the mere necessaries of life; of the husband's steadily increasing ill-health, physical and mental, ending in insanity and early death; of enforced migrations to Dresden and Düsseldorf in search of more lucrative posts for him as an orchestral conductor, and of the defeat of even these efforts by the incompetence of disease; and of the wife's loyal resumption of concert playing, in order to fill the family purse. All this experience of the sordid actualities with which the world always tests its idealists was well calculated to make even Schumann take a sober, and at times a tragic, view of life; and though

[1] "Clara Schumann, Ein Künstlerleben," by Berthold Litzmann, 1903–1906.

he is always noble and devoted, there is often in his chance remarks, as years go on, a note of weariness, melancholy, or philosophic resignation. It is not that he surrenders his ideals — only that he finds them more difficult of realization than he had supposed in the flush of youth, and under the buffets of fate retires somewhat into himself, and chastens his enthusiasm into a stoical faith and a more patient loyalty. This change of temper inevitably makes itself felt in such characteristic music as the solemn introduction and the aspiring adagio of the C-major Symphony, the mystical "Cathedral Scene" of the "Rhenish Symphony," the sombre and restless "Manfred Overture," the noble "Funeral March" in the Piano Quintet, and the infinitely tender Andante grazioso of the Piano Concerto. The same sincere, simple nature as ever is felt behind these things, but the stream of its emotion is now more profound and quiet, as a river, when it reaches the plains, no longer sparkles and bubbles, but flows tranquil and deep.

Technically, Schumann was handicapped in this new departure by his exclusively pianistic early training. He had acquired a habit of thinking in terms of the piano which it was almost impossible to break, and he had not, like most symphonists, familiarized himself with orchestral instruments from boyhood. The consequence was that he made many blunders in his first essays in instrumentation, and never scored with the ease, certainty, and effectiveness of a master. An oft-cited instance is the opening horn-phrase of the first symphony, originally written as at (*a*) in Figure VIII, in which form it is grotesquely ineffective on account of the muffled quality, on the horn, of the fifth and sixth tones, and changed only on second thought, after rehearsal, to its present form, (*b*).

Figure VIII.
Horns in B-flat.
(*a*)

(*b*)

Another is the first trio of the scherzo in the second symphony. Curiously oblivious of

tonal monotony, he cast this passage entirely
for the strings, despite the fact that they
had been prominent throughout the whole
of the preceding scherzo. It was Mendelssohn who suggested the use of the wood-
wind instruments here, certainly a marked
improvement. Isolated errors or miscalcula-
tions like these, however, are much less serious
than the pervasive heaviness and muddiness of
scoring that constantly mar the sound-mass.
A mistaken desire for richness of color led him
to double his instruments until all transparency
was lost. It is as if a painter should use all
his pigments all the time: the potency of each
would be cancelled by the others, and the eye,
through a surfeit of impressions, would become
dulled and jaded. Only by the silence of some
instruments can others come into relief. "Schumann's symphonies," says Mr. Weingartner,[1]
"are composed for the pianoforte, and arranged
— unhappily, not well at that — for the orchestra. Whenever I compare, as a conductor, the
labor of the rehearsals and the performance
with the final effect, there comes over me a

[1] "The Symphony since Beethoven," Eng. trans., p. 31.

feeling similar to that I have towards a person in whom I expected to find mutual friendship and was disappointed. No sign of life gleams in this apathetic orchestra, which, if given even a simple Mendelssohnian piece to play, seems quite transformed." There are, it is true, as Mr. Weingartner would doubtless admit, many single passages of great tonal beauty and originality scattered here and there in these overladen scores. Such are the sombre trombone harmonies at the end of the slow movement of the B-flat Symphony, the celestial violin melody in the adagio of the C-major Symphony (to which Mr. Weingartner gives the highest praise), and the violin solo in the Romance of the Symphony in D-minor. Above all, there is the wonderful horn-call in the "Genoveva Overture" — one of the loveliest moments in all music.

Figure IX.
Sehr frisch.

But these are the high lights in a picture which for the rest is too often gray and blurred.

In the chamber music, too, we feel the same shortcomings. The three quartets sound patchy or dry, like piano pieces played without pedal;[1] only in the quintet and the quartet with piano does Schumann's favorite instrument introduce elasticity and sparkle.

Another problem, even more fundamental than that of instrumentation, which Schumann, in approaching the larger forms, had to solve as best he could, was that of melodic variety and breadth. Here again he was at a disadvantage. All his experience had been with short lyrical melodies or germs of melodies such as are appropriate to piano pieces in the romantic vein and to songs; but larger works require a wider sweep in the initial themes, a more complex differentiation of themes, and a power of mental synthesis that can combine the most diverse elements in a coherent organism. Mr. Hadow[2] names the two types of melody,

[1] See the Adagio of the Quartet, opus 41, no. 1. The accompaniment is essentially a piano accompaniment, transcribed for 'cello and viola; but without the pedal it lacks fluidity.

[2] "Studies in Modern Music," First Series, Essay on Schumann, p. 213.

which are suitable respectively to the large and
to the small forms, the "Continuous" and the
"Discrete." "In the former," he explains, "a
series of entirely different elements is fused into
a single whole: no two of them are similar, yet
all are so fitted together that each supplies
what the others need. In the latter a set of
parallel clauses are balanced antithetically: the
same rhythmic figure is preserved in all, and the
differences depend entirely upon qualities of tone
and curve. The former is the typical method
of Beethoven, the latter that of Schumann."
And he cites as examples Beethoven's violoncello sonata in A, and the opening movement
of Schumann's piano quintet. Now, the
construction of extended works out of melodies
of the discrete or lyrical type presents certain
inevitable difficulties that the romantic composers, who instinctively think only in such
melodies, are always having to meet in one
way or another. We have already seen[1] how
Schubert, on the whole, failed to solve the
problem, and contented himself with monotonous repetitions of his ideas, or with variations

[1] Essay on Schubert, p. 98.

of their mere ornamentation or timbre. We shall later see how Chopin declined, and how Berlioz and Liszt evaded, the same embarrassment. It will be enlightening to examine how far Schumann succeeded and how far he failed in readjusting his musical imagination to the new requirements.

In many cases he fails as Schubert failed. Beginning a symphonic movement with a song-like melody, grouped in parallel phrases, generally of four measures' length, he is able to proceed only by more or less "vain repetitions." The result is a monotony, a flatness and lack of contrast and relief, something like that of a wall-paper with its endless re-presentations of a single pattern. This defect is especially felt in the development sections of his first movements and finales, in which he has, by the compulsion of circumstances, to forego the charm of melodic novelty. In the allegro of the first quartet, the development is founded on two or three patterns, many times reiterated in various keys. The first movement of the piano quartet, in spite of its harmonic originality, is open to the same criticism, as are also, in fact, most of the development sections in all four of the symphonies. A welcome contrast is found in the corresponding parts of the first movement in the quintet, where an ingenious "diminution" of the theme gives opportunity for much genuine variation, and of the finale of the concerto, with its inexhaustible fertility of rhythms and melodic figures. It must be added, also, that even when Schumann is most helplessly shackled to his initial themes, these are of such intrinsic beauty that the effect is infinitely to be preferred to that of more skilful mediocrity.

Next to the primordial charm of his melodies, his most efficient aid in the solution of the problem is his instinct for counterpoint, with all its matchless power to vitalize the musical tissue. This instinct was educated by a long and earnest study of Bach. As early as 1829 he made thorough acquaintance with the "Well-tempered Clavichord." In 1832 he writes: "I have taken the fugues one by one, and dissected them down to their minutest parts. The advantage of this is great, and seems to have a strengthening effect on one's whole system; for Bach was a thorough man. There is nothing sickly or stunted about him, and his works seem written for eternity." One of the most striking passages in the letters is that which acknowledges the supreme importance of such study to the romantic composers. "Haydn and Mozart," he says, "had only a partial and imperfect knowledge of Bach, and we can have no idea how Bach, had they known him in all his greatness, would have affected their creative powers. Mendelssohn, Bennett, Chopin, Hiller, in fact all the so-called romantic school, approach Bach far more nearly in their music than Mozart ever did: indeed all of them know Bach most thoroughly. I myself confess my sins daily to that mighty one, and endeavor to purify and strengthen myself through him." Besides this general purification and strengthening of his musical thought, Schumann found in Bach an invaluable anti-dote for his wayward, youthful subjectivism; for Bach is of all composers the most deeply and abstractly musical, the most thoroughly founded on natural tonal laws, the least infected with extraneous ideals and meretricious methods.

His art is wholly objective, quite universal; he makes no concession to vulgarity or to insensibility, and his taste is as exacting as his skill is impeccable. Technically, too, he gave Schumann, too long habituated to the narrow scope and rigid rhythmical balance of the lyrical forms, just the emancipation, the mental liberation and broadening, which he needed. The way of escape from the prosodic monotony of the song lies through polyphony, through the conceiving of music as a group or bundle of melodies each of which has its own vitality and its own provocation to fancy. Once the composer learns to follow each strand in this web, for its own sake, and to attain coherence by the persistence of characteristic motives of all types, rather than by a slavish alternation of phrase and equal counter-phrase, the creation widens in his view, and he writes with a hitherto undreamed-of elasticity.

The wholesome influence of the polyphonic or contrapuntal habit of mind makes itself felt very early in Schumann's works, even in the piano pieces of the first period. Oscar Bie detects its earliest manifestations in opuses

13 and 14, but it is certainly noticeable in the "Impromptus," opus 5. The very scheme of this work, which is a set of variations on a fixed bass quite as much as on the "Romance" of Clara Wieck, suggests the Bach standpoint. The dexterous weaving of motives in sections four and eight show the same spirit. Above all, the fugato in the finale, with its bold contour and its steadily cumulative sonority and thematic interest, and with its striking stretto (see the figure), not only gives evidence of minute study, but is a far from unskilful imitation of a great model.

Figure X.
Theme and Stretto from the Finale of the Impromptus, opus 5.

THEME.

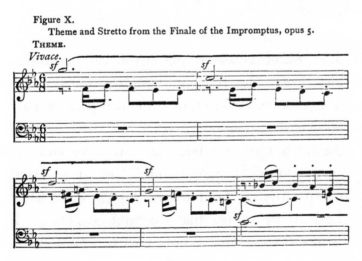

The habitual use of the sequence, the canon, and even the fugato, though always in an impressionistic, romantic vein, also presses itself constantly upon our attention. Such contrapuntal habits soon became instinctive and unconscious with Schumann. "In my latest compositions," he remarks in 1838, "I often hear many things that I cannot explain. It is most extraordinary how I write almost everything in canon, and then only detect the imitation afterwards, and often find inversions, rhythms in contrary emotion, etc." But the explanation is given by a sentence in the same letter: "Bach is my daily bread; he comforts me and gives me new ideas."

So beneficent in the small pieces, the inspiration of the Bach polyphony became invaluable in the larger works. To it are traceable the supreme passages in the symphonies, such as the profoundly thoughtful introduction of the C-major, with the rugged dissonances resulting from the superposing of the call of horns and trumpets upon the inexorable progression of the strings, the insistently climactic introduction of the D-minor, and the entire movement in the E-flat major known as the "Cathedral Scene," which is surely not the least of the monuments of Gothic art, though its massive pediments and soaring arches are carved of immaterial tones. In his three essays in the string quartet, the most exacting of all mediums, Schumann's contrapuntal skill is less secure. Failing often to conceive the inner voices independently, he falls into a jerkiness resulting from the constant stoppages of the little phrases; instead of letting the melodies germinate and soar, he constricts them within a predetermined harmonic mould; and the wall-paper patterns inevitably creep in. But in the quartet with piano and still more in the quintet, the contrapuntal stimulus is again efficiently felt. From the soaring imitations of the first page to the two exciting fugatos in the coda of the finale, one on the theme of that movement, and the other, by a happy inspiration, on the theme of the opening allegro, structurally rounding out the entire work, the music bubbles and throbs with melody.

One other great work there is, belonging to this period, which for fecundity of invention, luxuriant richness of coloring, and stoutness of structure deserves to rank with the quintet, if not above it. This is the piano concerto in A-minor, begun in 1841 and completed in 1845, — that is to say, written in the brief prime of Schumann's troubled life, when his powers had been marshalled and coördinated by discipline, and before they had become blighted by disease. It is thus quite up to his early standard in the matter of freshness of melody, rhythmic animation, and exotic gorgeousness of harmony, and at the same time far more firmly knit, more justly porportioned, and more flexibly conceived than the piano sonatas or the string quartets. The sincerity, tenderness, grace, and impetuous enthusiasm of the youthful romanticist are not in the least abated. What could be more contagious than the exuberant first movement, in which one hardly knows which to admire the more, the felicity of such details as the clarinet cantabile, the Andante expressivo for solo piano, and the nobly polyphonic cadenza, or the broadly climactic plan of the whole? What could appeal more simply and directly to the heart than the delicate and yet ecstatic Andante grazioso, with its winding intermeshed melodies, clustering about the violoncello phrases as a grapevine festoons itself upon a tree? Yet perfectly wedded with all this feminine suavity and grace is a more masculine quality, a fine poise, restraint, reservation of force, which counteracts all tendency to feverishness, and gives the work a sort of impersonal dignity

and beauty at the opposite pole from the perverse individualism of the "Davidsbündlertänze" and the "Carnaval." One feels that
the composer, no longer the victim of his
moods, is shaping his work with the serene
detachment of the artist. Particularly manifest
is this new mastery in the rhythmical treatment
of the finale. The rhythms here are as salient,
as seizing, as ever, but they are far more
various. The contrast between the strongly
"three-beat" quality of the initial motif, (*a*)
in Figure XI, and the cross accent of twos in
the second theme (*b*), is a stroke of positive
genius.

Figure XI.

Allegro vivace.

152

One should note also the subtlety with which
the regular three-beat meter is gradually re-
sumed after the interregnum (c in the figure).
Indeed, to do justice to the plastic beauty of this
movement would require nothing less than a
measure-by-measure analysis of its charmingly
varied phraseology. To play it after the
"Abegg Variations" is like passing from a
schoolboy's singsong delivery of "The Boy

Stood on the Burning Deck" to the reading of an ode of Shelley or a sonnet of Keats.

In our desire to comprehend how much Schumann gained by his study of Bach and other great masters of composition (such as his contemporary, Mendelssohn, for instance, whose perfection of form he vainly tried to emulate, possibly to the disadvantage of his own originality), we must not fail to note certain indications that his enthusiasm sometimes overleaped itself. A strong will like his easily falls, by the overuse or abuse of special artistic devices, into mannerisms; and he, with his fondness for sequences, inversions, canons, and other contrapuntal traits, did not escape this danger. So long as he used these tools with a certain romantic freedom and geniality, inspired by their spirit rather than enslaved by their letter, as he uses for example the canon in the andante of the piano quartet, the device of diminution in the development section of the first movement of the quintet, and the fugato in the finale of the same, they enriched and guided his fancy. But when he writes canonically throughout a whole movement, as in the scherzo of the

D-minor Trio or the third movement of the F-major Trio, when he puts upon his genius the manacles of strict counterpoint, as in the Studies in Canon Form for Pedal Piano, opus 56, and in the Four Fugues, opus 72, above all when he indulges, as in the organ fugues on B-A-C-H, in those inversions and retrogressions of themes dear to the schoolmen, then learning becomes baneful, and music degenerates into a pedantic exercise.

A far more insidious and fatal blight than such occasional pedantry was now, however, beginning to overspread his music. The story of the long, gradual eclipse and final extinction some years before death, by the ravages of physical and mental disease, of a genius which had dawned so brightly and reached its meridian in such ample and yet tempered splendor, is one of the most pathetic chapters in the history of art. The exact nature of the disease was somewhat obscure, but the basis of it seems to have been a tendency, inherited from the mother, toward abnormal activity of the brain, and a resulting congestion, distention of the blood-vessels, and final ossification of cerebral tissue, carrying with it mental paralysis and degeneration. The trouble was no doubt aggravated by overwork and by the constant excitement of musical composition. A peculiar feature was its reaction on Schumann's spirits. Generally this sort of cerebral atrophy is attended by unreasoning high spirits, a baseless self-satisfaction uncanny to observe but merciful to the sufferer. But Schumann's native moral force and mental power were so great that he struggled with his fate as a lesser man would not have done; and the result of the unequal fight was a terrible melancholy, sinking sometimes into a blank lethargy of depression, and rising at other times into acute despair. It was in one of these frenzied moments that, in February, 1854, he attempted to drown himself in the Rhine. Rescued from suicide, he had for safety's sake to be put in an asylum, where after two years of merely vegetative existence, he died on July 29, 1856.

This deep-seated physical disability is responsible for the curious impotence of those compositions which he so restlessly produced all through the afflicted years. Such things as the violin sonata, opus 121, the "Introduction and Allegro Appassionata," opus 92, the Concert Allegro, opus 134, and the overtures "Julius Cæsar," "Braut von Messina," and "Hermann und Dorothea," negligible from the artistic standpoint, are as human documents deeply pathetic. In them we see the crippled master in fruitless travail. The intention is always noble, the old fire flashes out now and then, the ideal of expression is the same as ever, but the path from will to act is clogged, the musical fancy is paralyzed; and all that results is page after dreary page of rigidly unchanging rhythms, stagnant harmonies, manufactured melodies, and climaxes that reach no goal. Particularly saddening is it to note the hysterical character of the emotional passages. In the overture to "Manfred," one of his immortal masterpieces, he showed once for all his marvellous power for impassioned expression. Alas! that in the fever of sickness he was goaded to parody his own immortal work in futile replicas that imitate its qualities only to trivialize them.

It is a relief to turn from the sorry spectacle of these galvanic twitchings of the once so virile intellect to the one happy episode that lightens this period of gloom. This was the coming of Brahms in 1853. In order to understand fully what the apparition of a youth of so pure and high a genius meant to Schumann, we must remember the depth and unselfishness of his love for art, the lifelong labors he had undertaken in order to purify public taste, the grim and often single-handed battle he had waged against Philistinism and mediocrity. Composition, the service of the gods of music at their inmost shrine, had been only one aspect of his life; the other side had been his literary and editorial labors, in which, like a true priest, he had gone forth to spread the faith among heretics and idolaters. The *New Journal of Music*, which he founded in 1834, had for its object, in his own words, "the elevation of German taste and intellect by German art, whether by pointing to the great models of old time, or by encouraging younger talents." "The musical situation," he wrote some years afterwards, "was not then very encouraging. On the stage Rossini reigned, at the pianoforte nothing was heard but Herz and Hünten;

and yet but a few years had passed since Beethoven, Weber, and Schubert had lived amongst
us. One day the thought awakened in a wild
heart, 'Let us not look on idly;. let us also lend
our aid to progress, let us bring again the poetry
of art to honor among men.'" The proposal
thus made, in a spirit of altruistic devotion to
art unhappily too rare among creative musicians,
was faithfully carried out in a series of apprecia-
tive, generally discriminating, and always enter-
taining articles on such men as Mendelssohn,
Gade, Bennett, Franz, Henselt, Heller, Berlioz,
Liszt, Thalberg, and Moscheles, alternating
with others of a more historical or general character, always wise, fair, suggestive, and pleasantly
pointed with humor, wit, and the play of that
irresponsible fancy which revelled in Jean Paul
and created the *Davidsbund*.

One of the most touching features of the
New Journal, to a reader of to-day, is the almost
too generous kindliness of its judgments, the
eager enthusiasm with which it proclaims the
advent of geniuses who have already fallen into
oblivion. Its editor proceeded so heartily on
the principle that it is wiser to encourage the

good than to discourage the bad that he often
"discovered" nonentities only to have them
left helpless on his hands. The experience
must have been disappointing to the most
sanguine. Seldom as he condemns, too, he
must frequently have had the petty egotists
swarming and buzzing about him, black flies
and gnats in human form, such as will beset
the stanchest crusader. To one engaged
in so humane and disinterested a task, and
pursuing it through such annoyances, the advent
of a true genius like Brahms must have been the
most joyful of events. Schumann at once
recognized and welcomed it. When Brahms,
then a tow-headed, high-voiced boy of twenty,
arrived from Hamburg with a parcel of manuscripts, he gave him, in the famous article,
"New Paths," the most royal greeting a neo-
phyte has ever received from a brother musician.
"He has come, the chosen youth, over whose
cradle the Graces and the Heroes seem to have
kept watch. May the Highest Genius help
him onward! Meanwhile another genius—that
of modesty — seems to dwell within him. His
Comrades greet him at his first step in the world,

where wounds may perhaps await him, but also the bay and the laurel." "It is a fitting reward," says Mr. Hadow, "that the voice which had so often been raised in commendation of lesser men should devote its last public utterance to the honor of Johannes Brahms."

Indeed, despite the struggles of his youth, the hardships and disappointments of his manhood, and the cruel affliction that maimed and killed him before his time, Schumann's destiny, look at it with but sufficient largeness, was a happy one. It is not given to men to attain their ideals; and in this respect, as in so many others, he was most human. His life, in its mere actualities, is, like all lives, a thing of incomplete beginnings, disappointed hopes, defeated or unrealized aspirations. But to look at the individual is to see but a partial, and therefore a distorted and misleading, picture. Only in his relations to others, in his service to the common good, in the seeds of social benefit which he plants and the ways of social progress which he discovers, is his true life to be found. If he has wrought faithfully, purely, single-mindedly, his work will suggest and imply more than it attains; and it will partake by virtue of this suggestion in all future attainment of the same kind. All Schumann's work tends in the direction of what is highest and most beautiful in music. Much he achieved, but much more he realized only as an ideal realizes that to which it points, and in some sense gives it solid reality in the world. Whenever and wherever men pursue what is pure, high, fresh, noble, and fair in music, there the spirit of Schumann will be at work.

IV

FELIX MENDELSSOHN

—

FELIX MENDELSSOHN
From the painting by Edward Magnus

IV

FELIX MENDELSSOHN

—

⚘

I N studying the relations of a number of contemporary artists to the general tendency of their age it is interesting to note how, in spite of the influence exerted upon them all by prevailing conditions and available opportunities, each responds to the occasion in his own way, always maintaining, in the common enterprise, his own particular ideals, tastes, and methods. Despite all the schools and movements in the history of art, each artist remains himself. So it was in the period of romanticism. The romantic tendency was in the air — the tendency to subjectivism, to picturesqueness, to specialized expression, to a richly sensuous embodiment of ideas; but nevertheless, each individual composer approached music from his own standpoint, seized upon those elements in it for which he had a native affinity, and quietly ignored what did not attract him.

That Mendelssohn should have been a romanticist at all is a proof of the strength of the romantic tendency in his day; he seemed born rather for the severest, purest, most uncompromising classicism; and if he did, as a matter of fact, come to share the ideals of his age, it was in his own way and for his own ends. The crudities, the exaggerations, the morbid self-involution of the extreme phases of the movement, certainly never infected him. For this happy immunity he was indebted largely to the fortunate conditions of his life, both personal and artistic. Crudity is usually a result of narrowness of culture or of a deficiency in technique; and Mendelssohn grew up in a singularly refined domestic and social circle, and was a skilled musician before he was breeched. Exaggeration springs from a lack of taste; and Mendelssohn's taste, both by native endowment and by training, was consummate. Self-consciousness, whether blessed or baneful, is the child of suffering; how, then, should it come to one whose whole life was so protected, so guided, so lapped in material prosperity, family affection, and social respect?

Mendelssohn's life reads like the story of some fairy prince, beautiful, brave, and virtuous, who is rocked in his cradle by the gentle godmother, Good-fortune, who runs his race amid the plaudits of admiring friends, and who dies young, untarnished, and full of honors, as one loved by the gods. He never knew the squalor of poverty, the paralysis of drudgery, the bitterness of inaptitude, the dull ache of disappointment. In his bright, precocious childhood he was the idol of a wise father, a fond mother, brothers and sisters who shared his tastes and in some measure his abilities, and a circle of literary and artistic friends at the head of which was the aged Goethe. In later years he had all the advantages of university training, the best teachers in music, foreign travel, varied friendships, a happy marriage, and a fame extending to all corners of Europe. Appropriately indeed was he named Felix.

The influence of a long-established, carefully bred, and highly cultivated family played an important part in the formation of his personality.

Schubert, Schumann, Chopin, Berlioz, and Liszt blazed out suddenly, meteoric individuals, from respectable but obscure origins; but Mendelssohn was the last bright flower put forth by an ancient stock. Only as such can he be understood. His grandfather, Moses Mendelssohn, an orthodox Jew of the old school and a self-made man, was a famous scholar in his day. He was prominent in the intellectual circles of Berlin in the middle of the eighteenth century, participated in a famous controversy with Lavater, was a friend of Lessing, and was the author of "Phædon, or the Immortality of the Soul," a work translated into all European languages. His son Abraham inherited his strong character and something of his mental power, without his genius. An independent thinker, an unusually wise and devoted father, he was yet singularly modest, and used to say that he began by being "the son of his father" and ended by being "the father of his son." He married Leah Solomon, daughter of a wealthy Jewish family of Berlin. It was her brother, a man of some reputation as an art critic, who, turning Christian, adopted and induced Abraham Mendelssohn to adopt the name of Bartholdy, as a distinction from the branches of their families which retained the ancient faith. Fanny Mendelssohn, Felix's sister, was also an unusual person. She had a genius for music second only to his, and would doubtless have become famous had it not been for her father's prejudice against a professional life for women. Some of the "Songs without Words" are of her composition, and her criticism was always eagerly welcomed by her brother. She married Hensel the painter, who added still further to the artistic interests and associations of the Mendelssohn family.[1]

In Felix's sixteenth year his father bought the mansion known as "Leipziger Strasse no. 3," in the suburbs of Berlin, which became the scene of a most idyllic family and social life. There were separate suites of apartments for the various groups of the clan, Fanny Hensel and her husband occupying one side, and her sister Rebecca and her husband, Edward

[1] See S. Hensel's "The Mendelssohn Family, from Letters and Journals," a fascinating book. English translation published in London, 1881.

Devrient, the other; there was a room suitable for theatrical performances, which were frequently given; there was a large garden, and in the middle of it a garden-house with a hall accommodating several hundred persons, in which informal musicales were arranged every Sunday afternoon. No pains were spared to grace the everyday life. "In the summer-houses," we read,[1] "writing materials were provided, and Felix edited a newspaper, called in the summer 'The Garden Times,' and in the winter 'The Snow and Tea Times.' To this all comers were invited to contribute, and the young people were joined in their fun by their elders, including such distinguished personages as Humboldt and Zelter." We can readily imagine that music was the constant accompaniment of all that went on; for not only did Felix and Fanny play the piano and compose, but Rebecca and her husband were singers, and Paul, the youngest of the family, was a good violoncellist. For the Sunday afternoon musicales Felix constantly wrote new things, of which the most important was the

[1] "Mendelssohn," by S. S. Stratton, p. 40.

"Midsummer Night's Dream Overture," played before a crowded audience in the garden-house at the end of 1826.

Had Mendelssohn not been surrounded, thanks to the wealth and cultivation of his parents, by this atmosphere of social friendliness and artistic charm, he might have had reason to regret the nervous sensibility he had inherited from them. The abnormal delicacy of constitution indicated by the fact that his grandfather, father, mother, and sister all died of cerebral paralysis took in him the form of such an excitability, physical, emotional, and mental, as would have brought much suffering upon a youth whose conditions of life had been less ideal. Extreme sensitiveness was the most radical trait of his character and temperament. His affection for his relatives was of passionate intensity; a slight misunderstanding or coolness would reduce him to tears, he could not work when his brother or sisters were ill, and the death of his sister Fanny was a shock from which he never recovered. His friendships were romantic in their ardor and in their exacting demands; he showed in them, indeed, the childish egotism of the oversensitive. "Write soon, and love me," he ends one of his letters; and a friend said of him, significantly, "He loved only in the measure that he was loved." [1] His brother-in-law, Devrient, in his reminiscences, says that when crossed or disappointed he sometimes lost all self-control, and in illustration tells the story of some theatricals planned for the silver-wedding celebration of his parents, for which he had written the music, and in which Devrient was to sing the principal part. At the last moment Devrient was summoned to sing at the Crown Prince's on the very evening appointed. With singular blindness to everything but his own plans, Mendelssohn begged him not to go, and when all were assembled began to talk incoherently, and in English. "The stern voice of his father," says Devrient, "at last checked the wild torrent of words; they took him to bed, and a profound sleep of twelve hours restored him to his normal state." It was the same sensitiveness, doubtless, that underlay his vanity in regard to his work, and made indifference so intolerable

[1] Compare what is said of Chopin at page 231.

to him. "The atmosphere of love and appreciation," says Devrient, "in which he had been nurtured was a condition of life to him; to receive his music with coldness or aversion was to be his enemy, and he was capable of denying genuine merit in any one who did so. A blunder in manners, or an expression that displeased him, could alienate him altogether."

But fortunately, at least for the moment, the cold winds of the outside world rarely invaded the quiet garden of art and friendship in which he passed his youth. Inside the barriers which his father's wealth and devotion, his mother's tender solicitude, and his sisters' comradeship and admiration reared about him, he composed, studied, and dreamed in idyllic peace. For variety there were conversations with men skilled in art and literature, studies in the classics and modern languages, harmless flirtations, letter-writing, water-color sketching, and tours in Italy and Switzerland. For recreation there were bowling, fencing, and swimming. And if the disagreeable could not be entirely eliminated, if there must be an occasional headache or fit of lassitude, or if, in spite of one's personal charm and graceful, lovable nature one's friends would not always take the trouble to understand one, then one could resort to a sort of Epicurean stoicism, refuse to attend to the painful and the annoying, and dwell insistently on all that was bright, gracious, and delightful.

Mendelssohn's earliest compositions reflect all the freshness and gaiety of his youthful nature, all the ease and charm of the circumstances in which it developed From the first their technical skill is perfect; for Mendelssohn had had no distracting struggles for daily bread, like Schubert, no moiling in arid, uncongenial studies, like Schumann; he had been placed under the best masters, and had assimilated harmony, counterpoint, and fugue as unconsciously as most boys assimilate reading, writing, and arithmetic. What was even better, their style was entirely individual; for the spirit of Ariel had never before been incarnated in a musician — or, if it had been, it had smothered under impeding conditions. In the scherzo of the octet written at sixteen there are all the Mendelssohnian traits: fluent melodiousness, correct harmony, carefully polished detail, and an inimitable delicacy, finesse, and lightness of style. "The whole piece," wrote his sister Fanny, "is to be played staccato and pianissimo, the tremulandos coming in now and then, the trills passing away with the quickness of lightning; everything new and strange, and at the same time most insinuating and pleasing, one feels so near the world of spirits, carried away in the air, half inclined to snatch up a broomstick and follow the aërial procession. At the end the first violin takes a flight with a featherlike lightness, and — all has vanished." [1] The last words are quoted from a stanza of the Walpurgis Night Dream in "Faust," of which it was Mendelssohn's intention to give a musical illustration : —

> "The flight of the clouds and the veil of mist
>   Are lighted from above.
> A breeze in the leaves, a wind in the reeds,
>   And all has vanished."

The same kind of intention was carried out even more brilliantly in the "Midsummer Night's Dream Overture," of which it is not

[1] "The Mendelssohn Family," p. 131.

too high praise to say that it is worthy of its Shaksperian inspiration. In the immaterial dance of the violins and the strange calls of the trumpets and wood-wind instruments, as if from some cloudy No-man's-land, of this wonderful work, conceived by a genius and executed by a master only seventeen years old, a new type of music is born.

It is worthy of remark that in neither of these works is there the slightest trace of the turgidity so often observable in youthful productions. On the contrary, one of their most prominent traits is a cool dispassionateness, as of the deliberate, detached artist, remarkable in so young a man. The more one studies Mendelssohn's music the more one becomes convinced that this cool dispassionateness is one of his fundamental qualities. Everywhere it reveals itself — in the suavity of his melody, in the purity of his harmony, in the smooth fluency of his part-writing. Violence of contrast, dramatic trenchancy of expression, the over-emphasis of hysterical eloquence, he punctiliously avoids; he is always clear, unperturbed, discreet, harmonious. The lavish sensuousness of Schubert, the impulsive sincerity of Schumann, are impossible if not distasteful to this Addisonian temperament; personal sentiment, self-revelation, the autobiographic appeal, he avoids as the purist in manners avoids a blush, an exclamation, or a grimace. If he is romantic in his love of the picturesque, in his sense of color, and in his fondness for literary motives, his emotional reticence is entirely classic. He is more observant than introspective, and his art is more pictorial than passionate.

Compare, for a moment, by way of illustration, the overtures "Manfred" and "Hebrides." Schumann's work is intensely human from the opening onslaught of syncopated chords to the final, deep-drawn sighs of the contrabasses. There is unassuagable desire in the melody so appropriately marked "In leidenschaftlichem Tempo," there is the very accent of a lover's longing in the beautiful Astarte theme. The music constantly rushes on into feverish excitement, only to expend its force and die away to tender sadness, whence in a moment it lashes itself again into new fury. From this so human world —

"Of infinite passion, and the pain
Of finite hearts that yearn "—

Mendelssohn transports us, in his "Hebrides," to an island set in a boundless expanse of the sea, where we watch only the rise and fall of great billows and hear the long sigh of the wind and the cries of sea-birds. The fierce dissonances of Schumann, his ceaseless modulation, his never resting movement, give place to clear ethereal harmonies, to high, pure trumpet calls, poising violin melodies, and the thin note of the oboe suggesting infinite distance, and to an undulating movement like the ebb and flow of winds and waves. These two works are typical. If Schumann is incomparable in his insight into the storm and stress of the human heart, Mendelssohn is one of the greatest of landscape painters.

What is true of the "Hebrides Overture" is in greater or less degree true of all Mendelssohn's compositions which can be called really successful. They charm us not by their personal appeal, their introspective veracity, as Schumann's so constantly do, but precisely by their freedom from personal bias their objective

truth, their universal interest. When he makes
us see the winds and waves of the "Hebrides
Overture," the marching pilgrims of the "Italian
Symphony," the dancing fairies of the "Midsummer Night's Dream" music, it is not as
through a temperament, but as in the white
light of pure imagination. It is such a view of
the world as some visitant from another planet
might get — some gentle, happily organized being, whose intelligence was unperturbed by
human passions and undistorted by practical interests. It is the view rather of a Tennyson than
of a Browning. "In the eyes of Mendelssohn,"
a keen observer has recorded, "there was none
of that rapt dreaminess so often seen among
men of genius in art. The gaze was rather
external than internal; the eye had more
outwardness than inwardness of expression."
What is said here of the physical eye might
with equal truth be applied to that mind's eye
with which the artist envisages his work. Mendelssohn's attention, we feel, was never engaged
with his own emotions, but played like a dis-
embodied spirit about the impressions he was
imagining. He himself is as elusive as the elves

and fairies he so loved to depict. He is always behind his work rather than in it.

The chief technical peculiarities of Mendelssohn's music, as we should expect in an art pursued in this spirit of cool and competent impersonality, are fluency, grace, and elegance. His melody, lacking to an unusual degree the suggestion of impassioned utterance, is more decorative than expressive — a sort of tonal arabesque, often exquisitely wrought, but curiously unexciting. There is no boldness in the physiognomy of his tunes; they conform closely to the average type of traditional German melody; and their charm is due to the neatness and facility with which they follow the paths of least resistance. His harmony is solid and correct, but hardly ever unconventional; he prefers an authorized to a novel progression, values clearness above richness, and treats dissonances with the utmost circumspection. His attitude toward modulation is conservative. Certain of his works, such as the "Scotch Symphony," with its endless A-minor and D-minor, have justly been charged with monotony, so fond he is of hovering gently about among a few closely related keys. In polyphony his ideal is smoothness of progression. Those daring momentary collisions between different voices, each progressing independently, which give Bach's fabric such a stoutness, he shrinkingly avoids. His part-writing is almost too conciliatory, too considerate of the prejudices of the ear; the natural roughnesses are all ironed out or glossed over. In a word, whenever he has a choice between the original and the established, he chooses the latter; he is too urbane to risk startling his hearer, and prefers to ingratiate himself with familiar charms; but so deftly does he manage these that he constantly gives us the pleasure of recognizing "what oft was thought, but ne'er so well expressed."

In the matter of orchestration his delicate ear and fine taste made him a great master. His instinct for proper balance and fusion of timbres is unerring, he knows how to be sonorous without becoming opaque or blatant, and his scores abound in the purest, clearest, and freshest colors. Where shall we find a parallel for that ethereal shimmer of the violins in the "Midsummer Night's Dream Overture," or for the magical chord of the wood-wind that arrests it? or for the serene beauty of the violin melody, so airily poised, at the end of the same overture? or for the liquid coolness of the flutes, violins, and trumpets in the "Hebrides"? or for the elastic vitality of the violins at the opening of the "Italian Symphony"? Here, we cry with delight, is a master who can make flutes and clarinets and violins in their upper register, and trumpets playing *piano*, sound not like mere orchestral instruments, but like angelic voices in remote skies. This magical charm is largely due to the limpid transparency of his coloring. He never overscores, never surfeits the ear and confuses the mind by laying on the tints too thickly or piling up colors that will not coalesce. Few composers have so fully realized how little an effect is due to the mere quantity of the sounds, how much to their skilful composition.[1] As an example may be cited the last page of the "Con moto moderato" movement in his "Italian Symphony," where the same motive is sounded first by horns and bassoons,

[1] Compare the remarks on Schumann's scoring, at page 139.

then by trumpets and drums, then by flutes and oboes, all together building up the loveliest, most diaphanous fabric of tone.

Figure XII.

An even more striking instance, remarkable both for the economy of the means employed and for the indescribable charm of the resultant effect, is the passage for violins and two flutes, in the "Pilgrim's March" of the same symphony.

Figure XIII.

Ending.　(Figure XIV)

As a master of pigments like Monet knows how to set on the canvas spots of pure color which merge only in the eye of the beholder, so Mendelssohn builds Æolian harmonies with a few pure tones that fill but never cloy our ears.

So long as Mendelssohn maintained his instinctive aloofness from human emotion, so long as, dwelling in his heaven of imagination, he painted delicate aquarelles of fairyland and romantic natural scenery, he was an incomparable master. In that rarefied atmosphere sentiments, like objects, were quite properly somewhat ghostly, tenuous, impalpable; the cheerful Mendelssohnian contentment sufficed for joy, the tender Mendelssohnian melancholy for sorrow. But as time went on it was perhaps inevitable that he, too, like Schubert and

Schumann, and indeed all sincere romanticists, should strive to leave his fanciful boyish world behind him, and to express something of those deeper realities with which the years were making him acquainted. Accumulating experience may well have brought to the man of forty a distaste for the gracious insubstantiality which was entirely charming in the work of a youth of seventeen. But, unfortunately, a serious difficulty presented itself at this point.

From the outset a thoughtful observer might have doubted whether so artificially protected a life as that of Mendelssohn's youth would develop his character and genius, in the long run, so favorably as it at first promised to do. There is such a thing as a good fortune so unrelieved that, by removing the prick of adversity, the challenge of obstacles, the illumination of sympathy, it becomes in truth misfortune. This is the fate that seems to have overtaken Mendelssohn. The smile of Destiny, constant from his youth, became at last fixed and vacuous. As in his boyhood he had been the pet of his family, so in manhood he became, as conductor of the famous Gewandhaus

Orchestra in Leipsic, and general dictator of musical affairs, the pet of a larger but still almost invariably indulgent circle. As his fame as a composer, conductor, pianist, and organist increased, the admiring audience widened until it comprised all Germany; and when in his last years he turned to oratorio writing he had England too at his feet. A wit has vividly pictured the atmosphere of adulation in which he lived in the remark: "Mendelssohn could not stick his head out of the window but some one would shout 'Hurrah!'"

The tendency of such an environment is to cramp the sympathies, smother the sense of humor, and intrench the petty pride of the most magnanimous of men; Mendelssohn was peculiarly at its mercy, because extreme sensitiveness inclined him to be wounded rather than enlightened by such adverse criticism as he got, because consciousness of real merit put him off his guard against the exaggerations of hero-worshippers, and because the innate bias of his mind was more toward a fastidious distinction than toward a rugged catholicity. Even in his youth his affections, as we have seen, were exclusive and jealous; and on the intellectual side a similar narrowness showed itself in a certain preciosity that we should call bigotry had it been less amiably expressed. That is a significant incident that Berlioz relates of his sojourn with Mendelssohn in Rome in their student days. "One evening," he says, "we were exploring together the Baths of Caracalla, debating the question of the merit or demerit of human actions, and their remuneration during this life. As I replied with some enormity, I know not what, to his entirely religious and orthodox opinions, his foot slipped, and down he rolled, with many scratches and contusions, in the ruins of a very hard staircase. 'Admire the divine justice,' said I, helping him to rise; 'it is I who blaspheme, and it is you who fall!' This impiety, accompanied with peals of laughter, appeared to him too much, it seemed; and, from that time, religious discussions were always avoided." The lack of plasticity here shown in a religious matter is also observable in his literary and musical opinions. Lampadius quotes his comment on Shelley's "Cenci": "No, it is too horrible! It is too abominable!

I cannot read such a poem." Mr. Hadow tells how he "praised the treatment of the double-basses in Berlioz's Requiem, just as he afterwards told Wagner that 'a canonic answer in the second act of "Tannhauser" had given him pleasure,'" and remarks, "There was always a little touch of Atticus in Mendelssohn's relations to his fellow-composers."

In the artificial air he was condemned to breathe, this pallor of intellectual anemia gradually became habitual. As a rare plant, kept always under glass, withers at a breeze which would invigorate the hardy weed so he could but shiver and shrink from those winds of impartial opinion which ruder natures inhale with zest. His youthful exquisiteness of taste thus grew peevish and fretful with advancing years. Too frequently we read of incidents like his studied coldness, throughout a long rehearsal, toward a favorite singer, and his curt explanation at the end: "Your curls provoke me, Fräulein Schloss. Wear your hair smooth; curls ought never to be black, but light brown or fair." Great, however, was the provocation. To set yourself a pace no mortal could maintain by writing the "Midsummer Night's Dream Overture" at seventeen; to marry an angelic creature who agreed with your most casual word and kissed your hand when you improvised in public; to move among admiring friends, relatives, pupils, and acquaintances as a king might move in a never ending triumphal procession; to find all qualms you might feel from time to time as to the superiority of your work immediately drowned by the immemorial habit of passive self-acceptance; to see other men, with other ideals, winning a success which your universally recognized fair-mindedness would not let you deny, — all this might bring pangs of bitterness to a saint.

Perhaps this spiritual and professional exclusiveness, and the isolation it resulted in, did not really grow with the years, but only seems more anomalous in age, which should be mellow, than in naturally arrogant youth. Certainly there were not lacking many evidences of a more wholesome development, of a growth toward larger ideals, of cordial services to fellow-artists. True self-respect, a very different thing from narrow conceit, is shown in the following passage from a letter. "As time goes on I think more deeply and sincerely of that — to write only as I feel, to have less regard than ever to outward results, and when I have produced a piece that has flowed from my heart — whether it is afterwards to bring me fame, honors, orders, or snuff-boxes, does not concern me." A fine modesty prompts the confession: "All I have done appears to me somewhat miscellaneous. . . . I know what ought to be, and is not." And in spite of the reserve that always impeded his social efforts, there is plenty of evidence that he put himself to much trouble to help such brother musicians as Liszt, Berlioz, and Spohr to gain a hearing.[1]

Above all, he was raised quite above all petty personal considerations by his whole-souled enthusiasm for the great ancient masters. His efforts to educate popular taste by familiarity with classical works were as unremitting and as disinterested as Schumann's. He was the most active of all the champions of Bach, at that time so shamefully neglected. His

[1] See the story of the banquet he tendered to Liszt in Leipsic, in Lampadius' "Life," p. 167.

performance of the great "St. Matthew Passion" in Berlin, in March, 1829, the first since the
composer's death in the middle of the eighteenth
century, is one of the most important events in
musical history; the significance of it, and of
his other labors in behalf of Bach propaganda,
to the entire subsequent progress of music,
and especially to the romantic movement, of
which Bach is one of the corner-stones, cannot
be exaggerated.

Yet, in spite of all this, if we compare
Mendelssohn with men like Beethoven, or
Schumann, or Tschaïkowsky, in whom feeling
is cordial and expression impulsive, we cannot
escape the impression of a certain thinness of
blood, straitness of sympathy, and inelasticity
of mind. His personality is tenuous, over-
rarefied; he seems more like a faun than a
man. And hence it comes about that when,
leaving his world of fairies, elves, visionary
landscapes, and ethereal joys and sorrows, he
tries to sound a fuller note of human pain and
passion, he is felt to be out of his element. His
style is too fluent, too suave, too insinuating and
inoffensive, to embody tragic emotion. It

lacks the rugged force, the virile energy, the occasional harshness and discordance even, of the natural human voice; its reading of life, in which there is ugliness, crudity, and violence as well as beauty, is too fastidiously expurgated. Which are the best of his piano works? Certainly not the "Songs without Words," with their facile melody, their monotonous rhythms and their cloyingly consonant harmony; nor the respectable, harmless, unexciting sonatas, cut from the same stuff, but by the yard instead of the square inch. Rather the "Variations Sérieuses" and the "Preludes and Fugues," in which there is some of the vigor of Bach, and the elusive immaterial whimsies, in the true Mendelssohn vein, such as the "Capriccio," opus 118, the scherzos, the "Spinning Song," the "E-minor Fantasie," and the "Rondo Capriccioso." Similarly, in the chamber music, it is the Canzonetta of the E-flat quartet, the scherzos of the trios, and the finale of the violin concerto, that most please us. As for the symphonies, even the noble adagio of the "Scotch" is just the least bit soporific; but the scherzo or the Scottish jig, and the fresh allegro vivace and stirring saltarello of the "Italian" are delightful. Mendelssohn gay and gracious is the best of company; Mendelssohn sentimental makes us "begin to loathe the taste of sweetness, whereof a little more than a little is by much too much."

The effeminate element in his work is probably chiefly responsible for the indifference, boredom, or distaste with which it is nowadays so often received. Since his romanticism was a matter of imagination rather than of passion, of fancy and delicate sentiment rather than of turbulent feeling, it is inevitably voted dull by a generation given over like ours to the pursuit of thrills, tolerant of any turgidity that can excite, and preferring intensity to clarity of emotion. He represents a mild, tentative, and restrained application of artistic principles that have been much more brilliantly and thoroughly illustrated by bolder spirits like Schumann, Chopin, and Liszt, who have accordingly somewhat eclipsed him. His conservatism also made him retain many of the traditional formulæ and mannerisms of classicism, which have become repugnant to our less conventional age. The result is that it has become almost a fashion to sneer or to smile at his music.   But it is conceivable that we err in one direction as much as his contemporaries did in the other.   It may be that we call his art stale and vapid merely because our palates are jaded by over-indulgence in spices and condiments.   Mendelssohn is undeniably, for the present, among the fallen gods; but whether a maturer and less sophisticated taste than our own may some day set him up again is a question we must be content to leave unanswered.

V

FRÉDÉRIC CHOPIN

—

FRÉDÉRIC CHOPIN

V

FRÉDÉRIC CHOPIN

CRITICS of literature and painting have succeeded in disseminating pretty widely the idea that the style of each artistic species is determined largely by the technical conditions under which it develops. We all know that one style is appropriate to engraving, another to oil-painting, and still another to pastel work; we recognize that the prose-writer and the versifier must use different vocabularies. Musical critics, however, whether from ignorance or from a disposition to involve their subject in an impenetrable haze of sentiment, have for the most part left us undisturbed to the enjoyment of our primitive notion that music, as a product of pure "inspiration," remains unmodified by such practical considerations as what voices can best sing, or instruments best play. We have to reach largely without their aid the conclusion that, in music quite as much as in literature or painting, the kind of body available to a composition determines in no small degree the sort of spirit which is to inhabit it.

The style of Palestrina, for example, the greatest master of the sixteenth century, bears the unmistakable stamp of the medium which at that time was firmly entrenched by tradition — the ecclesiastical choir of mixed voices. His polyphonic texture came in obedience to the necessity of making many melodies, simultaneous and intertwined, for the various groups of singers; the movement and range of his melodies were restricted by the rather narrow capacities of the human voice; his harmony, in the interests of accurate intonation, had to be kept simple and transparent. When, somewhat later, the organ came into vogue, it suggested certain modifications of style, splendidly realized by J. S. Bach. The natural capacities of the hands on the keyboard tended to focus attention quite as much on the chord as on the separate strands of melody, and the massive effects of chord-patterns began to vie in importance with the

more polyphonic traits. At the same time
harmony was free to become much more complex, since pipes cannot sing out of tune, and the
mechanically even tone, free from the *vibrato*
and incapable of the accentuation of voices,
made feasible a grand impersonality of style,
felt at its maximum in Bach's fugues. A little
later still the orchestra became the dominat-
ing medium, and Beethoven, ignoring altogether the ecclesiastical tradition, founded his
work on the secular dance and song, immemo-
rially associated with bowed and wind instruments. Melody became lyrical rather than contrapuntal, the exact balance of phrase by phrase
instead of the imitation of motive by motive grew
to be the chief means of coherence, and a systematic extension of this balance resulted in the
sonata-form. At the same time the marvelous
expressive power of the bowed instruments was
nobly utilized: on the emotional side music
became more than ever before profound, impassioned, mystical, and poignant.

As Palestrina, Bach, and Beethoven reflect
in their musical individualities the technique
of the chorus, the organ, and the orchestra, so

Chopin is in large measure a resultant of the peculiar qualities of the most influential of modern instruments, the pianoforte. This instrument had already assumed an important rôle during the life of Beethoven, and by the time of Schubert and Schumann it had made its influence deeply felt; but in no composer before Chopin do we find so delicate a divination of its capacities, so thorough a mastery of its mechanism, so willing an acquiescence in its limitations, so single-minded a formation of style upon the peculiar dialect it speaks in the language of music. Of none of his predecessors can it be said, as it can of him, that had the voice, the organ, and the orchestra not existed, his art would still have been essentially what it was. Indeed, his work is the offspring of so perfect a marriage between the artistic impulses of a sensitive human organism and the peculiar potentialities of a special instrument that it can be properly understood only through a study of both.

The most serious defect of the piano is its inability to sustain its tones. The tones of the voice and of wind instruments are limited in duration only by the air capacity of the lungs, those of bowed string instruments can be held indefinitely, and an organ pipe will sound as long as the air pressure is maintained in the bellows. The vibrations of a piano string, on the contrary, are at their maximum only during the moment in which it is struck by the hammer operated by pressing the key, and from that moment gradually decrease, giving forth a sound constantly fainter and fainter. Once the key is struck, the player's control over the mechanism ceases, and he has no choice but either to wait passively for silence or to strike another key. For this reason the broad, poising melodies and the slow-moving, deliberate harmonies of the choral and organ schools are ineffective on the piano. The long notes, fading momently away, fail, because of the insufficiency of their physical embodiment, to receive their due share of attention, and so lose their musical value. Still more do purely polyphonic passages, which depend for their effect on the leisurely succession of dissonances and their resolutions, subtly interlinked, suffer from the discontinuity of the piano tone. The indifference, or even insensibility, to the beauty of pure line, which characterizes so much of our modern musical taste, is probably in large measure due to the prevalence of an instrument so little suited to exhibit it.[1]

At a very early period after the piano came into common use, musicians began to recognize the necessity of minimizing its characteristic defect by modifying their manner of writing. They soon discovered that if the tones would not sustain themselves, they must be struck over and over again as rapidly as possible: repetition must counteract evanescence. An early application of this principle is the use, by Bach and other clavichordists, of trills, mordants, and other ornaments as a means of keeping long melody-notes audible. A more important one is the breaking up of chords into figures of short notes in the accompaniments of Haydn and

---

[1] Bach's " Well-tempered Clavichord " is an example of a work to which, since its beauty is largely one of line, the piano cannot do justice. See, for instance, Prelude IV, in C-sharp minor, in the first book, measures 4–7, inclusive. The tenor part, of a wonderful nobility, is concealed by the more rapidly moving, and therefore on the piano more sonorous, soprano. In order fully to bring it to our consciousness we must sing or otherwise reënforce it.

Mozart, a device which soon became so indispensable that a glance at any modern piano score will discover hundreds of such groups of short notes, which are nothing but chords played piecemeal in order to make them sound.

Figure XV.
(a) Mozart : Piano Sonata, A-major.

(on the chords)

(b) Beethoven: Piano Sonata, Op. 2, No. 3.

(on the chords)

(c) Schubert : Fantasia, Op. 15.

(on the chords)

(*d*) Chopin: Nocturne, Op. 55, No. 2.

(on the chords)

A melody in the right hand, accompanied by
these broken chords in the left — this soon became the normal texture of music intended for
the piano.

The first great merit of Chopin was that he
carried to its logical extreme this system of coun-
teracting the piano's defective sonority. The
great advance made by him is shown even in the
brief quotations of Figure XV. The Mozart
example is rudimentary — the device at its
lowest terms. In the Beethoven passage the
chords are placed too low; they sound muddy,
opaque, inelastic. In the Schubert passage the
sonority is better, but the figures are so arranged
as to be very difficult to play, on account of the
wide jump the hand has to make at the middle
of each measure. Chopin, on the other hand,
avoids muddiness by clustering his harmony

fairly high (about the region of middle C), at the same time gets a sufficient bass for his chords, which he is able to do by covering a great deal of ground in each figure, and in spite of the wide space traversed on the keyboard respects the comfort of the player by not requiring any sudden leaps. It is furthermore worthy of note that by introducing two tones foreign to the harmony (the fourth and the sixteenth) he gains a richness of sound lacking in the other examples. We get here, however, but the merest inkling of the inexhaustible ingenuity with which he manages this matter of "figuration," or the ornamental disintegration of chords. In order really to appreciate it we should have to examine those nocturnes, say, like the second, third, seventh, and eighth, in which with the left hand unaided he supplies a good firm bass and an intricate texture of accompaniment; we should have to study those pieces, such as the first, fifth, and eighth of the Études, opus 10, and the Prelude, opus 28, no. 23, in which it is the right hand that, racing back and forth over the keyboard, fills in the chinks of the harmony as a painter "stipples" an even tint with an infinite number of tiny brush-strokes; we should have to analyze in detail such a masterpiece as the Étude in A-flat major, opus 25, no. 1, in which it is both hands that weave together a diaphanous web of sound, while the outer fingers of one sing the tune, and those of the other the bass.[1]

Chopin's negative merit of minimizing the disadvantages of his instrument is, however, very intimately connected with a more positive skill in utilizing its peculiar advantages, in order to understand which we shall have to revert for a moment to our examination of the mechanism of the piano. The most characteristic feature of this mechanism — a feature so vital that it has been called the soul of the piano, and so unique that no other instrument except the harp pre-

---

[1] Schumann reports of Chopin's playing of this étude: " It would be a mistake to suppose that he brought out every one of the little notes with distinctness; it was more like a billowing of the A-flat major chord, swelled anew here and there by means of the pedal; but through the harmonies were heard the sustained tones of a wondrous melody, and only in the middle of it did a tenor part once come into greater prominence amid the chords, along with that principal cantilena."

sents a parallel to it — is the damper pedal, generally known by the inaccurate and misleading name of "the loud pedal." Its function is to raise all the dampers which control the vibrations of the strings, leaving them free to respond to any impulse they may receive. It thus secures two important results.

In the first place, it counteracts the non-sustainment of single tones by fusing a great many such individual tones, separately produced, into one impression. It will readily be seen, for instance, how indispensable is the pedal to the intended effect of the broken chords of Figure XV: only through its coöperation do they become worthy equivalents, in the piano idiom, of what the organ or voices would present in the form of sustained chords in long notes. Moreover, every tone sounded on the piano, with the pedal down, is reënforced, through what is known as sympathetic vibration, by many other tones not sounded by the hands at all. For, since every tone produced by a piano string is in reality, as proved by scientific analysis, by no means simple, but a complex of many elements known as "partial tones," and since any elastic body capable of producing a given tone will actually produce it, through sympathetic vibration, whenever the tone is already being otherwise sounded in its vicinity, it will readily be understood that all the partial tones set going by striking a piano key will, if the dampers are, by means of the pedal, kept from interfering, start into activity whatever strings are tuned to their respective pitches. Thus the pedal turns the entire body of strings into one vast Æolian harp, ready to take up, reëcho, and multiply the slightest breath of sound produced through the keyboard.

Some idea of the extraordinary enrichment of timbre or tone-quality which accrues to the piano through the sympathetic vibration made possible by the pedal may be gained by striking a single key, say middle C, first without, then with, the pedal. The first tone stands out hard and angular, like a leafless tree in a desert; the second is liquid, murmurous, palpitant, its outlines softened as a landscape is softened by a misty atmosphere. When a chord rather than a single key is struck, the effect is, of course, multiplied in direct proportion

to the number of its constituent tones. The hard
nucleus of the impression is clothed in a soft web
of subordinate sounds, the result of sympathetic
vibration. Suppose, for example, we play the
chord of four whole notes in Figure XVI. If

Figure XVI.

at the same time we free the strings by pressing
the pedal, we shall summon from them an
attendant train of ghostly "harmonics" for
each of the four, represented in the figure by
quarter-notes. These auxiliary tones, to be
sure, will be exceedingly faint and individually
indistinguishable, but they will nevertheless
give to the impression that curious mellowness,
depth, or liquidity (one calls vainly on the divers experiences of other senses to describe it)
which is one of the fundamental charms of the
piano tone.

The second important result of the damper
pedal is a still greater richness of tone

which it enables composers to attain by artificially pushing still farther the fusion of many
single tones which is illustrated on the plane of
nature by the foregoing examples. The student of harmony will observe that though most
of the "harmonics," written in quarter-notes, of
Figure XVI, are consonant to the fundamental
chord, and thus enrich without obscuring it,
there are several, notably the G-sharp, which,
being foreign to the chord, tend slightly to blur
its clarity. These dissonant harmonics are,
however, so faint that their effect is practically
nil. But if the composer, acting on the hint they
give him, introduces into his chords similar
foreign tones, sounded more distinctly by the
hands, he at once imparts to the harmony a
curious opacity and thickness which it is almost
impossible to describe, but which affords a pleasant contrast to the uniform clearness of purely
consonant chords. The fourth and the sixteenth notes in the bit of Chopin already cited
(Figure XV) illustrate this device. The effect
of such dissonant tones may be likened to the
effect of mixtures and body-colors in painting;
they afford relief from the monotony of con-

sonance just as those afford relief from the monotony of the pure colors. They provide the musical picture with chiaroscuro and atmosphere, softening the sharpness of its lines, spreading over it, so to speak, a delicate translucent haze. Used to excess, of course, they make a mere smutch, a meaningless, chaotic daub; the music reverts to primitive noise; the nice point is to use them just enough to gain depth, solidity, light and shade, without blackening and confusing the whole impression.[1]

Now Chopin is one of the supreme masters in the coloristic use of the dissonance. His nocturnes, especially the first, seventh, eighth, and fourteenth, may fairly be said to inaugurate by this means a new era in music, comparable in many respects to the era of impressionism in painting. Their tremulous, vaporous harmonies seem to come from no common piano, but from some wind-swept Æolian harp. Take, for instance, such a passage as the following, at the end of the third nocturne:—

[1] Of course, the amount of dissonance acceptable is not a fixed quantity, but increases as the perceptive power of the ear develops.

Figure XVII.

Here it is as if, after placing on his canvas the two main chords of the cadence, dominant and tonic, he took, while the colors were still wet, a brush, and with the softest imaginable touch drew it across the entire face of the picture. The grace-notes, most of which, it will be noted, are dissonant to the main harmony, are no more meant to be heard individually than the spots of paint in a Monet are meant to be seen individually; they are a running of the colors, blurring the otherwise too bald outline. Chopin's scores are full of these delicate veilings and obscurations. In a majority of cases they are produced, as in this instance, by the right hand, above a clear harmony in the lower register. But sometimes, more daringly,[1] he assigns the web of dissonance to the left hand, in the middle register or even in the bass, thus gaining an extraordinary lurid gorgeousness of coloring. The passage in the third ballade, beginning at the change of signature to four sharps (Figure XVIII), is an instance.

Figure XVIII.

[1] More daringly, because the lower the pitch of a dissonant tone, the greater the number of its audible harmonics, and hence the greater the degree of its obscuration of the harmony. Even a consonance, such as the major third, sounds "muddy" when placed in the lower register. Readers interested in this matter should consult some convenient handbook of acoustics, such as Broadhouse's "The Student's Helmholtz," on the subjects of harmonics or partial tones, sympathetic vibration, etc., and Mr. Arthur Whiting's "Pedal Studies," for a highly suggestive discussion of color in piano music.

And
later:

etc.

Or again, as in the "Meno mosso" of the
Scherzo, opus 39, both hands first deliver
bold, clear chords, and then weave a shimmer
of light above them.   In all such cases, it is
obvious that the dissonances in question do
not belong to the essential melodic and harmonic lines of the composition; they are, as
Mr. Hadow says, "effects of superficies, not
effects of substance," and may be compared
to those local blurs made by a draughtsman's
stump in a charcoal sketch, or, as before

suggested, to those surprisingly rich mixed tints produced in impressionistic paintings by a multitude of minute brush-strokes.

The at first sight very elaborate modulations of Chopin which have provoked so much discussion are but a further application of the same principle. They are really not modulations at all, in the classic sense of transitions from one key to another having a structural value, but rather amplifications of the groups of grace-notes that constantly embroider the tunes. Their function is sensuous rather than structural, and we might describe them by coining the word "grace-chords." Of the twelfth measure of the second nocturne, for example, Mr. Hadow well says that "when we see it on paper it seems to consist of a rapid series of remote and recondite modulations, but when we hear it played . . . we feel that there is only one real modulation, and that the rest of the passage is an iridescent play of color." Another striking instance is the following measure in the "Polonaise-Fantaisie," a composition in which effects of this sort abound.

Figure XIX.

The pedantic scholiast would say that the composer here modulated, with startling speed, through the keys of B-flat, C, D, and A-minor; but all that the mind grasps is the two chords at the beginnings of the measures, connected by a gorgeous pageant of inarticulate sound. The sketch is being rubbed with the draughtsman's stump again, this time with even finer temerity and more splendid result than before.

It is a lesson in the meaning of that much-abused word "originality" to observe that Chopin arrived at all these novel effects, which differentiate his style so strikingly from those of the conservatives and the virtuosos of his day, simply by discerning through a superior sensitiveness, and working out with a matchless skill, the peculiar potentialities of the medium at his hand. Realizing as no one else had done that the piano compensates for its inability to bring out the beauties of pure line (due to the non-sustainment of single tones), by the wealth of color made available through the pedal's fusion of many tones, both consonant and dissonant, in one composite impression, he shrewdly arranged his campaign accordingly. He adjusted all his technical resources, both as a composer and as a pianist, in the interests of the greatest possible transfusion and intermixture of impressions. This is the secret of his harmonic scheme, so chromatic and full of dissonance; of his lavish melodic embroidery; of his *tempo rubato*, by which the outline of meter itself, so arithmetical and inexorable, is gently relaxed; of his curious soft, light touch, which seemed to glide over rather than strike the keys — "so insinuating and gossamer a touch," says an ear-witness, "that the crudest and most chromatic harmonies floated away under his hand, indistinct yet not unpleasing"; and this is the secret of his lavish use of the damper pedal, equalled, among his contemporaries, only by that of Schumann.[1]

[1] It is, however, interesting to note that, lavish as Chopin's use of the pedal seems when compared to the general

The unprecedented individuality of the style he thus developed profoundly impressed all observers. "In the marvellous art of carrying and modulating the tone, in the expressive, melancholy manner of shading it off," says Marmontel in his "Pianistes Célébres," "Chopin was entirely himself. He had quite an individual way of attacking the keyboard, a supple, mellow touch, sonorous effects of a vaporous fluidity of which only he knew the secret." "Imagine," writes Schumann in the *New Journal of Music,* "an Æolian harp that had all the scales, and that these were jumbled together by the hand of an artist into all sorts of fantastic ornaments, but in such a manner that a deeper fundamental tone and a softly

practice of his time, the fondness for the turbid and cloudy colors produced by commingled dissonances has grown so rapidly that to-day we prefer sometimes even more pedal than he gives us. In the Ballade, opus 52, during that brilliant passage which debouches into the simple chords in B-flat major, modern taste would prefer a continuous pedal through six measures, instead of through only three, as Chopin has directed. We should also blur the eleventh Étude more recklessly than he does, and many other instances will occur to the reader.

singing higher part were always audible, and you have an approximate idea of his playing." Liszt's testimony is that he "imprinted on all his pieces one knows not what nameless color, what vague appearance, what pulsations akin to vibration," and that "his modulations were velvety and iridescent as the robe of a salamander."

Nor do the scholastic musicians of the time fail to pay this pioneer the eloquent tribute of misunderstanding him. Moscheles, a man of the old *régime*, writes, after hearing him play, "The harsh modulations which strike me disagreeably when I am playing his compositions no longer shock me, because he glides over them in a fairylike way with his delicate fingers." This comment is most significant. Moscheles found Chopin's modulations harsh because he played them with the punctilious accuracy, the absolute literalness, which is appropriate to the music of line, but not to the music of color. In rendering a Bach fugue we cannot get each tone too distinct, since it is sure to be a part of some melody, a clear perception of which is necessary to our appreciation of the design. But Chopin's polyphony is not Bach's polyphony, as is illustrated by the former's Prelude, opus 28, no. 1. Both the right- and the left-hand parts here are melodic; but if both are played with an equally salient touch, the conflicts between the voices become unpleasant. The proper way is to let the lower part sink into the background, giving merely a certain depth and opacity to the general impression; the two melodies are as it were on different planes, the lower one more remote and heard but dimly as through a slight haze. So it is everywhere in Chopin. To play him too distinctly is as fatal an error as to examine a charcoal sketch with a magnifying glass, or to bend over a canvas of Monet and peer curiously at each spot of paint. One must stand off, and half close one's eyes, until the details are lost in the masses. In a word, here is a new type of art, demanding a new mode of apperception. If a Bach fugue and a Mozart quartet are the steel engravings of music, Chopin's pieces are its impressionistic paintings and pastels.

But it is time to pass to some other phases of the extraordinary sensibility and unerring taste of Chopin, thus evidenced by his originality in technique, as they showed themselves in his everyday life and in the more intellectual aspects of his art. The chief events of his short career may be very summarily recounted. Born in Zelazowa-Wola, a small village in Poland, in 1809, he studied music in Warsaw, and at twenty-two established himself as a pianist and teacher in Paris, where he passed most of his life. In 1837 ill health, which soon developed into the pulmonary disease of which he died, compelled him to seek a warmer climate, and he passed the winter in the island of Majorca with George Sand, the eminent novelist, and her children. Thus began a connection which lasted for ten years, and which has given rise to endless discussion. The true inner history of this love-affair will probably never be known, as the evidence is fragmentary and distorted by prejudice. It is obvious, however, that neither the composer nor the novelist (whose real name was Madame Dudevant, but who had obtained a divorce from her husband before she met Chopin) was sufficiently unselfish to sustain permanently such a

relation; nor were their temperaments fundamentally congenial. They separated in 1847.
By this time Chopin's consumption was far
advanced, and after two more years of extreme
feebleness, complicated by poverty, he died at
Paris, October 17, 1849.

In physique Chopin was slender and of
middle height, fragile even before disease had
wasted him, but supple and elastic; his hands
and feet were small, his gestures varied and full
of grace; with his pale, almost sallow, complexion,
his long, fine, chestnut-brown hair, parted at one
side, his high aquiline nose, limpid yet bright
eyes, and sweet half-melancholy smile, he impressed Moscheles as "exactly like his music,
tender and *schwärmerisch.*"[1] Liszt says that
the timbre of his voice was subdued, and that
his movements had such a distinction and his
manners such an impress of good society that
one treated him unconsciously like a prince. In
the matter of dress he was as fussy as a woman,
sparing no pains (to the friends who served
him in these affairs) to secure just the distinguished mean between the insignificant and the

[1] *Schwärmerisch* — visionary, imaginative, dreamy.

ostentatious. "I forgot," he writes from No-hant, George Sand's country estate, to his friend Fontana, "to ask you to order for me a hat from my Duport, in your street, Chaussée d'Antin. Let him give the hat of this year's shape, not too much exaggerated, for I do not know how you are dressing yourself just now. . . . Call at my tailor's, on the Boulevards, and order him to make me at once a pair of gray trousers — something respectable, not striped, but plain and elastic. Also a quiet black velvet waistcoat, but with very little and no loud pattern, something very quiet but very elegant. Should he not have the best velvet of this kind, let him make a quiet, fine silk waistcoat, but not too much open."

Another letter of the same time amply proves the truth of his biographer's statement that he had the "*coquetterie des appartements.*" "Select wall-paper," he directs, "such as I had formerly, dove-color, only bright and glossy, for the two rooms, also dark green with not too broad stripes. For the anteroom something else, but still *respectable*. If there are any nicer and more fashionable papers that are to your liking, take them. I prefer the plain, unpretending, and neat ones to the shopkeeper's staring colors. Therefore pearl-color pleases me, for it is neither too loud nor does it look vulgar." In his later years, as health waned, the habit of luxury grew upon him. Near the end, just before leaving London for home, he writes another of his willing servitors, this time his friend Grzymala: "Please see that the sheets and pillows are quite dry, and cause fir-nuts to be bought; Madame Étienne is not to spare anything, so that I may warm myself when I arrive. I have written to D—— that he is to provide carpets and curtains. I shall pay the paper-hanger at once after my arrival. Tell Pleyel to send me a piano on Thursday; let it be closed and a nosegay of violets be bought, so that there may be a nice fragrance in the *salon*. I should like to find a little poesy in my rooms and in my bedroom, where in all probability I shall lie down for a long time."

The same fastidiousness is discernible in his musical and intellectual tastes. Liszt says that he ranked Mozart above all other masters, "because Mozart condescended more rarely than any other composer to cross the steps which separate refinement from vulgarity." "Yet,"

adds Liszt, "his sybaritism of purity, his appre-
hension of what was commonplace, were such
that even in 'Don Giovanni' he discovered
passages the presence of which we have heard
him regret." Next to Mozart came Bach,
whose works were the only music he carried
with him to Majorca, and whose exquisitely
lucid style exercised an important formative influence on his own. His pupil Mikuli says it
was difficult to tell which of the two composers
he loved better. Beethoven he accepted only
with reservations. "Certain parts of Beethoven's
works," says Liszt, "seemed to him too rudely
fashioned. Their structure was too athletic to
please him; their wraths seemed to him too vio-
lent." Mendelssohn he considered "common";
of Schumann's "Carnaval" he remarked that
it was not music; Meyerbeer and Berlioz he
heartily disliked, though for different reasons;
Liszt, according to Niecks, he often found
"guilty of making concessions to bad taste for
the sake of success," a sin which he "viewed
with the greatest indignation." On the other
hand, he liked the music of Bellini and Rossini,
on account of its southern suavity and grace.

Chopin took slight interest in philosophy and literature, and detested argument, whether political or religious. "Of universality" says Niecks, "there was not a trace in him;" and the composer Stephen Heller, himself a man of marked cultivation, pronounced him "uneducated." What little we do learn of his reading, however, is most characteristic. His friend Gavard, who read to him, in his last illness, out of Voltaire's "Dictionnaire Philosophique," remarks: "He valued very highly the finished form of that clear and concise language, and that so sure judgment on questions of taste. Thus, for instance, I remember that the article on taste was one of the last I read to him." The graphologist will supplement these bits of evidence with the testimony of his handwriting, inimitably neat and small. His manuscripts are marvels of penmanship: the notes like pinpoints, the slurs mere filaments of spider's web, the stems painstakingly vertical, even the erasures ornamental latticework, so that the whole is as much a drawing as a writing.

The least pleasing of all the manifestations of Chopin's exquisiteness is seen in his social habits. Here his refinement, his shrinking aversion to all that was crude, ugly, or grotesque, his sybaritic love of ease and elegance, made of him an ultra-aristocrat, a *précieux*,—one is often tempted to say, in good round English, a "snob." Dazzled by the brilliance and poisoned by the perfume of those *salons* to which his talent gave him access, his taste, so unerring in matters of art, failed to distinguish between the genuine aristocracy of mind and the spurious aristocracy of wealth and fashion. It is at once pathetic and exasperating to see such a genius, of whom an honest, simple man like Delacroix could say, "he was the most true artist I have met," anxiously striving to be borne aloft by that *haute volée* which was so immeasurably beneath him, limiting his society to that small section of humankind which proudly styled itself "*le monde*," and dedicating his leisure and his compositions, not to brother artists, but to the baronesses, countesses, and princesses who gave him their half-patronizing homage.[1] In his letters one too frequently comes upon passages like

[1] Three of his pieces are dedicated to baronesses, nine to countesses, and four to princesses.

this, from Vienna: "I have pleased the nobility here exceedingly. As a proof I may mention the visit which Count Dietrichstein paid me on the stage," or this from Paris, on his first arrival: "I move in the highest society — among ambassadors, princes, and ministers."

There is in the "Lettres Parisiennes" of Madame de Girardin a description of a *soirée* at Madame de Courbonne's, which brings this whole nauseous atmosphere with painful vividness under our very nostrils. "It was for passionate admirers," writes Madame de Girardin, "the torment of Tantalus to see Chopin going about a whole evening in a *salon*, and not to hear him. The mistress of the house took pity on us; she was indiscreet, and Chopin played, sang his most delicious songs; we set to these joyous or sad airs the words which came into our heads; we followed with our thoughts his melodious caprices. There were some twenty of us, sincere amateurs, true believers, and not a note was lost, not an intention was misunderstood; it was not a concert, it was intimate, serious music such as we love; he was not a virtuoso who comes and plays the air agreed upon and then disappears; he was a beautiful talent, monopolized, worried, tormented, without consideration and scruples, whom one dared to ask for the most beloved airs. . . . Madame So-and-so said, 'Please, play this pretty nocturne dedicated to Mdlle. Stirling.' — The nocturne which I called the dangerous one. — He smiled, and played the fatal nocturne. 'I,' said another lady, 'should like to hear once played by you this mazurka, so sad and so charming.' He smiled again, and played the delicious mazurka. The most profoundly artful among the ladies sought expedients to attain their ends: 'I am practising the grand sonata which commences [*sic*] with this beautiful funeral march,' and 'I should like to know the movement in which the finale ought to be played.' He smiled a little at the stratagem, and played the finale of the grand sonata."

Decidedly, there is too sickly a flavor of the boudoir about the *salons* in which "this beautiful talent . . . whom one dared to ask for the most beloved airs" deigned to spend his time. We cannot wonder that in such a hot-house atmosphere the ugly weeds of his character throve almost as well as the delicate flowers, that under such long-continued coddling he grew vain, captious, pettily egotistical. It is distressing to note how much he is willing to ask of his friends Fontana and Grzymala, in the way of laborious and disagreeable commissions — errands to tailors, landlords, paper-hangers, and furniture-makers, and bickerings with publishers — and how he is content to repay them with a few perfunctory protestations of regard, nicely proportioned, in each case, to the magnitude of the favor exacted. Nor does he hesitate to speak slightingly, behind their backs, of such associates as Pleyel the publisher, Leo the banker, and even his fellow-countryman Matuszynski, at the same time that he is addressing them directly in the most cordial and even affectionate language. In short, it is impossible to deny that he was exacting, ungenerous, and disingenuous in his relations with comrades and friends.

In the more casual relations the same shortcomings revealed themselves in a malicious wit which was quite devoid of the magnanimity and exuberance of humor. His description of

Thalberg, his rival as a virtuoso, is a little masterpiece of irony: "He is younger than I, pleases the ladies very much, makes potpourris on 'Masaniello,' plays the *forte* and *piano* with the pedal but not with the hand, takes tenths as easily as I do octaves, and wears studs with diamonds." When Liszt, who in the consciousness of his splendor was inclined to patronize, volunteered to write a review of one of his concerts, he said, "He will give me a little kingdom in his empire." To a wealthy Philistine who invited him to dinner, and as soon as the coffee was removed requested him to play, he responded sweetly, "Ah, but I have eaten so little!" Obviously Liszt is right in describing him as "a fine connoisseur in raillery and an ingenious mocker."

But just as the sneer is physiologically the incipient uncovering of the teeth, in self-defence, of the animal at bay, so Chopin's sarcasms are the retaliations of a man constantly harassed, upon a dull and cruel world. He had to resort to innuendo because he was too fragile for rougher warfare. The needles of his wit had to be sharply pointed and dipped in venom, to make any impression on people accustomed to fight with sledge-hammers. All his weaknesses of character, indeed, — his malice, his extreme caution, his secretiveness, his vanity, even his snobbishness, — are in large measure but the necessary reflexes of inherent weaknesses of constitution, and may be explained, if not altogether condoned, as the normal reactions of a too sensitive nature, placed without protection in a sordid, difficult, phlegmatic world. Never, surely, was human being more delicately adjusted than Chopin to receive painful impressions at every point. His senses were so keen that as a child he cried at the mere sound of music; disease made him shrink from minute changes of temperature or slightly unfavorable conditions of weather, of which ordinary people are unconscious; imperious pride made him similarly susceptible to his social climate; and his high artistic ideal condemned him to constant disappointment even with his work. Peculiarly pathetic is the story of the last year of his life, when, unable to compose or to teach, almost penniless, and so weak that he had to be carried upstairs by his valet, he

undertook an ill-fated concert tour in Scotland
and England. It was a sad jest of destiny to
bring this subtle artist, dying of consumption,
into contact with a Manchester audience, in a
large hall which his tone could not fill. He
begged his friend Osborne not to be present —
"My playing will be lost in such a large room,
and my compositions will be ineffective." Hueffer describes a similar scene in London, a Grand
Polish Ball, at which "the people, hot from
dancing, who went into the room where he
played, were but little in the humor to pay
attention, and anxious to return to their amusement. He was in the last stage of exhaustion,
and the affair resulted in disappointment."
It was an excusable bitterness with which, on the
way back to Paris, pointing at the cattle by the
wayside, he murmured "Ça a plus d'intelligence
que les Anglais." But, alas! to a temperament,
like his, too delicately strung, the whole world,
always and everywhere, is somewhat British.

The single, but perhaps sufficing, good
fortune in Chopin's in many ways unhappy lot
was that he was able to find a refuge from the
irritations, failures, and disappointments of

everyday existence in artistic expression. However stubborn an aspect life presented to him, in art at least he was successful. The great law of compensation never wrought more subtly than when it made the very qualities which defeated him in the one realm the sources of his joyful conquest in the other. The keenness of sense which found in the hurly-burly of the world so many painful impressions, also discovered, as we have seen, wonderful new possibilities of tonal coloring in pianoforte music. The minute discrimination which made him unpleasantly conscious of all that was vulgar, crude, and ugly in human nature, also enabled him to winnow out unerringly, from his musical resources, all trite formulæ, all hackneyed conventional progressions, all threadbare adornments, and so to attain a marvellous individuality and distinction of style. The very exclusiveness which condemned the man to solitude, safeguarded the artist against dissipation of energy and futile eclecticisms of method. Finally, his ideal of perfection, a cruel autocrat to serve in a world so imperfect, proved the best of guides in the less refractory medium of art, and led him near to the verge of complete realization. In a word, the paradox of Chopin is that his fastidious taste — the radical, fundamental trait of his nature — plunges him, as a human being, into a jungle of distresses, but guides him, as a musician, to a mountain-top of commanding superiority.

The unfailing interest of the analysis of his music lies in the recognition, at every turn, of this fineness of nature, this mental and spiritual high-breeding, this exquisitely sensitive taste, and in the detection of the various kinds of excellence it produces. One easily traces it through several planes of achievement, in an ascending series. On the first and lowest plane it appears merely as an inimitable finesse in the execution of light, playful, and even frivolous designs: no one has brought so delicate and yet firm a touch, and so sure an instinct for dainty elegance of style, to the treatment of the *salon*-piece (a *genre* for which we find perhaps the best parallel in the paintings of Watteau or the verses of Mr. Austin Dobson) as the Chopin of the waltzes, the mazurkas, many of the études and preludes, and even of the more old-fashioned concert fantasias and *" variations brillantes.*" Weber is as polished, but less subtle; Schubert is as spontaneous, but by no means so distinguished. Schumann exerts the same fascination, but with less ingratiation, less *politesse;* Liszt's musical garment is equally sparkling, but it is gemmed with rubies rather than with diamonds. The technical sources of Chopin's success in this *genre* are his graceful, smoothly-moulded melodies, frequently recalling those of Bellini and other Italians, with whom he had much in common; his simple, transparent harmonies, built up always with an unfailing sense of tone-color; and his lambent, coruscating ornamentation, which always seems to effloresce spontaneously from the melody. In all these matters he is the supreme model of purity and felicity in this style.

But the same punctilious taste which guided him so safely among the pitfalls of virtuosity and bravura soon led him beyond this entire scheme of art, which is, after all, based on the somewhat frivolous ideal of ostentation, up to the higher level of lyrical expression, based on quiet and deep personal feeling. The virtuoso was transformed into the poet. In the nocturnes, some of the études and preludes, portions even of the ballades and polonaises, and most strikingly of all in the slow movements of the concertos and sonatas, his object is no longer to dazzle his audience, but to portray subjective emotion, often of a profound earnestness and spiritual beauty. If in his early pieces he was the prestidigitator, the brother-in-art of Thalberg and Liszt, here he is the dreamer, the rhapsodist, and his nearest of kin is Robert Schumann. The largo of the B-minor Sonata is Schumannesque in its contemplativeness, its *innigkeit*, its marked note of mysticism; the funeral march in the B-flat minor Sonata equals that of the great quintet in poignancy and dignity, though it is a feminine version of what in the German composer we find expressed with more virile force. In the nocturnes the feminine quality is even more evident. Their tender beauty has a pallor, a fragility, almost an emaciation, which has often brought upon them the charge of morbidity. It is certain that in the pieces of this type Chopin has carried his fastidiousness a stage farther than in the display pieces, attaining an even greater distinction and a rarer individuality. The nocturnes and preludes, the larghettos of the two concertos, the largo of the Sonata in B-minor, and a few other things of the same sort constitute one of the few perfect manifestations of the romantic spirit in music.

There is still a third phase of Chopin's work, which some will probably consider as much higher than the lyrical phase as that is higher than the decorative. This may be called the heroic or epic phase, and is exemplified in the polonaises, the ballades, the Fantasie, opus 49, the twelfth étude, the thirteenth nocturne, and the finale of the Sonata in B-minor.[1] A study of these works will open the eyes of any one who knows Chopin only through his virtuoso or lyrical pieces to the scope and many-sidedness of his genius. There is about them a largeness of utterance, a sustainment of mood, an intensity of emotion hardly ever degenerating into the hysterical or the sentimental, which it is strange to find in the graceful *salon* writer, the delicate miniaturist. Yet this final quality, too,

[1] It is noteworthy that most of these compositions bear opus numbers higher than 40, and belong to the last decade of the composer's life.

by which Chopin proves himself akin to Beethoven as well as to Thalberg and Schumann (an oddly assorted trio), is, like the others, due to his characteristic fineness of nature. It is the heroism of high breeding, the vigor of intelligence, the dignity of impeccable taste. It bespeaks a strength rather subtle than brutal — the strength of the mettlesome thoroughbred, not that of the stolid dray-horse. It is a spiritual superiority (like the technical and emotional superiority) born of distinction and nourished by exclusiveness. Even in the most virile of the polonaises, with the possible exception of the so-called "Military Polonaise," which is unique in its fresh, open-air athleticism, we feel that the power which surges through them is a nervous rather than a muscular power. Thus when he is heroic, no less than when he is gay or introspective, Chopin remains true to his slender, aquiline, subtle, aristocratic self.

It is interesting to examine the evolution of technique that went hand in hand with his growth in emotional earnestness. In the first place the Bellini-like tunefulness, illustrated in the theme of the Rondeau, opus 1, with its agile

turns and trills and its skipping staccato movement, gives place in the maturer works to a
freer, more chromatic, more impassioned and
rhapsodic type of melody. It recrudesces, to
be sure, here and there, as in the ninth nocturne, the larghetto of the E-minor concerto, the
moderato cantabile of the "Fantaisie Impromptu"; for the languid southern luxuriousness was once for all a part of Chopin's
temperament. But the deeper and more intimate the mood he is trying to express, the broader
and less trammelled becomes his melodic curve.
How sinuous the line, how gradual the climax,
how deliberate the subsidence, of this theme
from the fourteenth nocturne (*a*, in Figure XX)!

Figure XX.

(*a*)

How majestically the phrases rise, tier on tier, in the chief melody of the Polonaise, opus 44! How nobly rhapsodical, how genially spontaneous and flexible, is the phraseology of the second theme in the allegro of the B-minor Sonata (*b*, in Figure XX)! Well may Mr. Edward Dannreuther call Chopin "the supreme master of elegiac melody."

In his greatest tunes Chopin indeed touches
a point which few purely romantic writers
ever reach. We have noted, from time to
time, in the course of these studies, the tendency
of all lyrical composers to build up their music
out of a few short phrases many times repeated,
like the patterns in a wall-paper; we have seen
how Schubert, Schumann, and Mendelssohn
fell into this pitfall even in their orchestral
works, which therefore, in comparison with
Mozart's or Beethoven's, seem patchy, breathless, or monotonous. We have seen that melodies of "long breath" are conceivable only by
minds of sufficient synthetic power to entwine
many phrases, diverse in length, contour, and
rhythm, into a single organism. Now Chopin,
like the rest, writes only too often in the "wall-
paper" style, as may be seen especially in the
waltzes, mazurkas, and nocturnes. But at other
times he shows a synthetic faculty rare among
lyrists, by which he attains a noble breadth.
Look, for example, at the passage marked
"sostenuto" in the Grande Valse, opus 42, at
the surging bass theme of the Polonaise, opus
40, no. 2, or at the second theme of the allegro

of the B-flat minor Sonata, noting the sustained flight of the second eight measures of the tune. Better still, examine with some particularity, studying the diversity of the rhythmic figures employed, the two melodies in Figure XXI, one from the Ballade, opus 23, and one from the finale of the Sonata, opus 58. Mark the

Figure XXI.

deliberation, the suspension of interest, of the sequence in measures 5–8 of the first, the exciting inevitability of the chromatic descending scale near the end of the second.[1] In such tunes as these, which are frequent in his later works, Chopin proves himself capable of the veritable *"longue haleine"* of the epic melodist.[2]

A second technical result of the gradual deepening of Chopin's ideal of expression was a wonderful development of his harmonic sense. In the works of his prime he is one of the greatest of all masters of expressive harmony. His originality in modulation and enharmonic transition,

[1] Cf. also the subsequent, even more extended, treatment in the sequel.

[2] It may be asked why, possessing this enviable *longue haleine*, Chopin did not turn it to better advantage in writing his sonatas and concertos, which are structurally not satisfactory examples of their types. In answer it may be suggested (1) that in the concertos he was hampered by the orchestra, his technique being essentially pianistic; and (2) that his melodies, however broad in scope, are generally lyrical in character, and hence not adapted to symphonic treatment. With his characteristic caution, however, he used these most extended forms but sparingly; and in the more rhapsodic long forms, such as the polonaises and ballades on a large scale, he is highly successful.

his employment of chromatic progressions
cheek by jowl with passages based on the old
diatonic modes of the Polish folk-music, his
daring use of consecutive fifths and other such
bugbears of the scholastic, entitle him to a high
place among the pioneers of modern methods.
He constantly surprises us with premonitions of
Liszt, Wagner, the French and Russian composers of to-day, and even Richard Strauss.
Thus, for instance, the opening of the great
Polonaise-Fantaisie, with its constantly shifting tonality, its groping bass, its murky, mysterious minor-ninth and diminished-seventh chords,
seems like a page from "Tristan"; the series of
kaleidoscopic modulations, marked "stretto,"
near the end of the fourth ballade, recall Tschaïkowsky in one of his most reckless moods;
and we must go to César Franck to find a parallel
for the lapsing chromatic dominant-seventh
chords of the twenty-first mazurka.

Nor does Chopin make the mistake, so
fatal to some modern writers, of surfeiting our
ears on these complexities until they become
apathetic. His taste is too sensitive for that.
Scarcely are we launched on an admiring study

of his harmonic intricacies (which it must be confessed became in his latest pieces, as Mr. Niecks suggests, almost too fine-spun) before we are arrested by some fascinating bit of utter simplicity and bell-like clarity. How grateful, after the ominous harmonics at the beginning of the Polonaise, opus 26, no. 2, in the lower register, the restless seventh chords of the principal tune, and the clanging dissonances above the pedal-point on F at the middle of the first section — how grateful, after all this clamor and stridency, are the triads and dominant sevenths of the Meno mosso (see Figure XXII). It is as if

Figure XXII.

sotto voce.

ten.

some bright band of pilgrims marched, to the clear peal of trumpets, out of the dust and blood of a battlefield. Exquisitely beautiful, again, is the celestial purity of those chords, transparent and colorless as crystal, which are introduced near the beginning of the second impromptu: —

Figure XXIII.

Other similar passages are the "religioso" section in the sixth nocturne, and the middle section of the eleventh, both of which, in their ecclesiastical serenity and severity, take one back to Palestrina. And with all his diversity of vocabulary, Chopin never confuses his effects. He can pass from the extreme plainness of the fifth étude to the chromatic complexity of the sixth, without the least adulteration of either.

Why the works of a master so various yet
always so elevated in style, animated by so high
an ideal of what it is worth while to say, and of
how it should be said, should be specially marked
out for sentimentalization and degradation at the
hands of performers too dull to divine their distinction, is one of the mysteries of perverse destiny. It is hard to see what justification can be
found, either in the internal evidence of the
works themselves or in the recorded opinions
of their composer, by the misguided enthusiasts
who drag out his lovely melodies into mawkish
recitatives, break his chords into arpeggios, and
vulgarize his *tempo rubato* into license of meter
and confusion of rhythm. There is, to be sure,
in much of his music, a subjective quality, an
intimacy of mood, which gives the debauchee
of sentiment an opportunity he does not find
in abstract classic art. There are even a few
instances, to give him countenance, of actual
affectation, the tiresome posturing of the "dramatic" tone-poet, as in the pompous ending of
the ninth nocturne and the theatrical opening
of the third scherzo, where Chopin seems to
borrow a gesture from his friend Liszt. But the

entire object of the foregoing analysis will have
been missed if it has not convinced the reader of
the essential distinction, the superiority to all
claptrap eloquence and feverish emotion, of
Chopin's mind. He was not a man to strut and
pose; he was too busy with an artistic ideal, too
bent upon expressing a high vein of feeling in a
faultless technical medium.

There is also plenty of documentary evidence to prove his abhorrence of all sickly sentiment, and of the messy technique it induces.
Take, for example, the matter of the much discussed *tempo rubato*. Chopin regarded this as
a sensitive adjustment of time values, a delicate
elasticity or flexibility of pace — by no means as
a departure from essential metrical accuracy.
"The left hand," he said to his pupil Von Lenz,
"is the conductor; it must not waver or lose
ground; do with the right hand what you will
and can." "He required adherence," says another pupil, "to the strictest rhythm, hated all
lingering and dragging, misplaced *rubatos* and
exaggerated *ritardandos*. 'Je vous prie de vous
asseoir,' he said on such an occasion, with gentle
mockery." His aversion to melodramatic ex-

pressiveness, in which the artist surrenders himself weakly to a momentary excitement, may be inferred from his remark on Liszt's performance of a Beethoven sonata: "Must one, however, always speak so declamatorily (*si declamatoirement*)?" and from a comment on his own playing by Cramer, a pedant who, without entirely comprehending him, yet could not but discern the dignity of his art: "I do not understand him, but he plays beautifully and correctly, he does not give way to his passion like other young men." Finally, if Chopin had really been a mere voluptuary and sentimentalist, is it likely that he would have composed with such concentrated intensity of labor? "He shut himself up in his room for whole days," writes George Sand, "weeping, walking, breaking his pens, repeating and altering a bar a hundred times, writing and effacing it as many times, and recommencing the next day with a minute and desperate perseverance."

No, Chopin may not be a giant like Bach, or Mozart, or Handel, or Beethoven, but he is a sincere and earnest artist, who feels vividly, and spares no pains to give his feelings worthy expression, and to attain a supreme plastic beauty. Above all, he is a man of the most delicate sensibility, the most discriminating taste, the most exacting ideal of artistic perfection. In leaving him, it is pleasant to attend less to the sufferings to which these qualities condemned him as a man, than to the achievements to which they led him as an artist. This shifting of emphasis is what he would himself have desired, for his aspirations and standards were æsthetic rather than ethical; he lived as he could, it was only in composing that his will was free and efficient; his very individuality takes definite shape only in the favoring medium of musical imagination and emotion. In that firmament of music he will continue to shine, a fixed star, not perhaps of the first magnitude, but giving a wondrously clear, white light, and, as he would have wished, in peerless solitude.

VI

HECTOR BERLIOZ

—

HECTOR BERLIOZ

VI

HECTOR BERLIOZ

—

OT many years ago three Americans, coming, late one afternoon, in the course of a walking tour in northern France, to the little cathedral town of Beauvais, found its ordinarily quiet air filled with tumult, bustle, and confusion. The streets, gay with colored bunting and venders' booths, were thronged with crowds of merrymakers; the hum of insatiable conversation was everywhere; no rooms were to be had at the hotels, and their dining rooms were preëmpted by crowds of men in uniform, engaged in an endless round of toasts and speeches. Beauvais was, in a word, the scene of a "Grande Fête des Pompiers," or Firemen's Festival. The firemen of all the surrounding country had assembled there, had taken possession of the town, and had surrendered themselves to conviviality and joy. It was a spectacle interesting from many points of view; but the fancy of the American observers was most of all struck by certain long strips of bunting which spanned the streets at intervals, bearing in large letters the legend, "Honneur aux victimes du devoir." This, it seemed to them, was the note in this motley symphony most perfectly, inimitably, and deliciously French. These festive firemen, in the midst of their jollifications, did not forget for a moment that it was their proud privilege to stand before the world, so long as cognac allowed them to stand at all, as the honored victims of duty. One hardly knew whether to smile at their ingenuousness, or to thrill in sympathy with their emotion, which, however theatrical, was perfectly sincere; on consideration one did both.

Something of the quandary of these American observers of the very Gallic firemen of Beauvais must perhaps always be experienced by the Anglo-Saxon who tries to understand the French attitude toward life or art, so essentially different are the two types of temperament. It is hard for the stolid, matter-of-fact, insensitive, self-satisfied Anglo-Saxon, singly set upon his business, indifferent to what the world may think of him, to comprehend the subtleties and indirections of the Gaul, who conceives personal conduct as an actor conceives a rôle, spares no pains or labor to do justice to his part, and feeds on the applause or starves on the indifference of his audience. To your Englishman or American such an ideal seems trivial, artificial. His sense of humor, a faculty in which it must be confessed that the French, for all their wit, are deficient, seizes at once upon the incongruities that must always exist between an ordinary human life and a histrionically conceived rôle, and in his amusement he often fails to do justice to the intelligence, imagination, and courage that may be brought into play by such a dramatic exercise. Possibly to a higher point of view his own attitude, which he likes to call "practical," and which less friendly critics sometimes call stupid, might seem essentially no better than the playful chivalry of his fellow.

Such thoughts as these are bound to occur to the candid critic of that singular man, that quintessential Frenchman, Hector Berlioz. On first acquaintance he seems a creature of postures and pretence, grandiloquent, artificial, specious. He resorts to any means to make an impression, keeps his name before the public by journalism, by social eccentricities, by Byronic love-affairs, by all manner of ingenious indirect advertising, thrives only in the smile of the public, and writes much less to express an inner conception of beauty than to dazzle, startle, and stun. He seems to make a religion of idiosyncrasy, and to shrink from nothing but the natural. He lives, speaks, writes, composes, only in the interest of his carefully laid plot to be unprecedented. But then, as one studies him more, one begins to find admirable traits under this fantastic exterior. However artificial his ideal may be, he brings a most vivid and many-sided intelligence to its service; in spite of the opposition to the world in which his excessive individuality places him, his stock of good-nature and of half-ironical, half-kindly wit is inexhaustible; and if he does not worship at an orthodox shrine, he can suffer, and endure, and strive, like a true martyr. And so Berlioz's critic, like the Americans at Beauvais, finally decides to smile at and at the same time to admire him.

Hector Berlioz, born December 11, 1803, at La Côte St. André, a small town in southeastern France, began his long struggle with the world when, in his nineteenth year, in Paris, whither his parents had sent him to become a doctor like his father, he resolved to abandon the study of medicine for that of music. It was a daring, indeed a rash, resolve, worthy of a born dissenter like Berlioz; for not only were all external forces clearly in league to keep him in the beaten path, but his vocation for music was as yet far from obvious. He played only the flageolet, the flute, and the guitar; his knowledge of harmony was of the slightest; and he himself tells us in his autobiography that he had never seen a full score, but that one day when he found a sheet of paper ruled with twenty-five staves he "realized in a moment the wondrous instrumental and vocal combinations to which they might give rise, and cried out, 'What an orchestral work one might write on that!'" The impulse was there, if the technique was wanting; and when the young medical student chanced to hear a performance of Gluck's "Iphigénie en Tauride," his smouldering enthusiasm burst at once into unquenchable flame, and he resolved at all hazards to become a musician.

He introduced himself to Lesueur, professor of composition at the Conservatoire, with a cantata in which there were many blunders in harmony, but a good deal of dramatic power also, and on the strength of it became his pupil. He studied the scores of Gluck's operas in the Conservatoire library. With characteristic audacity he proposed to the aged Andrieux, lecturer on literature in the school of medicine, that he should write for him an opera libretto, but received a courteous refusal. He did not hesitate to borrow twelve hundred francs from a friend as a means of producing at the church of Saint-Roch a mass he had written. And all this time he was raising obstacles for himself by his enthusiastic impulsiveness and his utter lack of tact and worldly discretion. The story of his first meeting with Cherubini, a man of far-reaching influence as the director of the

Conservatoire, will serve as an example. Cherubini, who was a cold and formal precisian, had made a strict ruling that the male and female readers at the Conservatoire library should enter by different doors. Berlioz "did not see the notice," entered by the women's door, and immediately buried himself in the score of "Alceste." Presently he was recalled to this world by finding Cherubini standing beside him, "a thin, cadaverous figure with a pale face, tumbled hair, and fierce, gleaming eyes." Then arose an angry altercation, ended by the director's ordering the porter to eject the offending student, and a lively chase among the desks. Berlioz, reaching the door, only stopped to announce to the enraged Cherubini that he was "soon coming back to study Gluck again." He did so; but he never conciliated the ill-will of his powerful enemy, who from that day lost no opportunity to frustrate his ambitions.

It was indeed his failure to win one of the Conservatoire prizes, which lost for him the countenance of his parents and plunged him into many misfortunes. His mother at this time threw him off entirely, in anger for which there was much justification; his father, more patient, allowed him a period of probation, after which, if he could not show himself a successful musician, he was to return to the study of medicine. Thus put upon his mettle, he rented a closet of a room up five flights of stairs, lived on bread, raisins, prunes, and dates, and eked out his allowance by taking pupils on the guitar and the flute, and in solfeggio. In this way he even managed to pay half of his debt to the friend who had helped him produce his mass. But alas! this man, as careless and devoid of tact as Berlioz himself, then wrote to the father the story of the loan, requesting a payment in full. Who can wonder that Dr. Berlioz, his toleration at last exhausted, upon paying the balance of the debt cut off entirely the allowance? Not even then, however, would Berlioz accept defeat, but, getting a post as chorus singer in one of the small theatres, continued the struggle to attain the prize on which so much depended. Could he but gain the *Prix de Rome*, he would be assured an annuity of three thousand francs for five years, the first two to be spent in the French Academy at

Rome, the third in Germany, and the last two at home: he would be free to study and compose at leisure, he could show the world and his parents what was in him.

The subject prescribed for the competition in 1826 was the death of Orpheus, on which he proceeded to wreak himself with an ardor we can well imagine. The result was that his bacchanal scene was pronounced unplayable by the mediocre pianist provided to play the pieces to the jury. Berlioz was furious — and most of all, characteristically, at the injustice done his orchestration. "The piano," he cries, "at once reduces all composers to the same level, and places the clever, profound, ingenious instrumentalist on the same platform with the ignorant dunce who knows nothing of this branch of his art. The piano is a guillotine, and severs the head of noble or of churl with the same impartial indifference." As the time of the next trial approached, Berlioz with his usual impolitic frankness made such a nuisance of himself, by criticising in a loud voice, from the pit of the opera house, the liberties taken with the scores of the great masters, that he was debarred altogether by the scandalized authorities. In 1828, missing the first prize by two votes, one of them Cherubini's, he obtained the second prize, consisting of a laurel wreath, a not very valuable gold medal, and a free pass to the opera-house. Still invincible, he prepared himself to storm once more the pedantry of the judges; he did his best, but, in the words of Boïeldieu, "they found his best too good," and in 1829 the prize was not awarded at all. It was not until 1830 that, at last learning by experience, he wrote his cantata of "Sardanapalus" in the dryest and most conservative style he could compass, leaving out altogether the conflagration scene, which might have proved unplayable, and at any rate would have disturbed the tranquillity of the judges. Discretion won the day; the prize was awarded him, and he was free to depart for Rome, and to finish his cantata to his own satisfaction, which we may be sure he lost no time in doing.

In the meantime, as if these struggles were not enough to engage all his energies, he had been busy playing the first scene of that love-tragedy, or melodrama, or farce — one hardly

knows what to call it — which ended by join-
ing him in uneasy and brief wedlock with
Henriette Smithson, an Irish actress. It is
hard to tell how far the throes of his very
Gallic heart were genuine, how far they were
manufactured by his susceptible fancy, his
literary imagination, and his keen sense for
dramatic effect. There is ever about Berlioz a
trace of the little boy playing pirate chief; he
goes through life with something of that youthful ecstasy of make-believe; and when he tells
us of his passions for Mdlles. S——, R——,
and M——, when he enumerates his thrills,
commemorates his tears, and confides his plans
for capture, flight, suicide, or double murder,
we wonder whether he really felt all this, or is
merely convinced, as a poet and journalist, that
he ought thus to have acted.

It was in 1827 that Berlioz first beheld his
future wife, who was acting Shakspere at the
Odéon in a troupe of English players. Of the
effect of her Juliet upon him he writes, "After
the third act, hardly breathing, in pain as if a
hand of iron were squeezing at my heart, I
said to myself, with the fullest conviction: 'Ah!

I am lost.'" Did he make any attempt to meet the lady whose beauty and genius had so singularly affected him? Not he; such a course would have been painfully commonplace, a terrible descent from poetry to prose. He followed her about with gaunt eyes and dishevelled mien, so that, believing him mad, she asked her friends for protection. He lost himself in melancholy revery, he roamed about the streets at night, in such despair that on one occasion Liszt and Chopin followed him, fearing he might kill himself. Then he rallied his forces in a great resolve; he would win his indifferent mistress by his art; he would give a concert of his own works, and she should hear it. "I will show her," he cried, forgetting in his enthusiasm that she had no ear for music, "that I too am an artist." After heroic labors and economies (for it was at this time that he was supporting himself by singing in the theatre chorus, and he had to work sixteen hours a day copying instrumental parts), after endless struggles with his conductor, who did not understand the music, and with Cherubini, who refused him the only available concert hall, he succeeded in bringing off the concert, only to find that Miss Smithson did not hear of it at all. Shortly afterward she left France for some years.

Disconsolate, Berlioz turned for comfort to a certain Mademoiselle Mooke, to whom he became engaged in 1830, soon after winning the *Prix de Rome*. This affair, however, went little more smoothly than the other, for hardly had he arrived in Italy before he received a letter from Madame Mooke, informing him that her daughter had married M. Pleyel. His rôle was thus suddenly changed to that of the abandoned lover, thirsting for revenge; and it must be conceded that he entered upon it with his usual artistic enthusiasm. "Two tears of rage started from my eyes, and my mind was made up on the spot. I meant to fly to Paris, where I had two guilty women and one innocent man" — one sees that magnanimity was a part of the rôle — "to kill without mercy. As for killing myself afterwards, you can well believe that that was indispensable." Behold him, then, in Florence, supplying himself with two double-barrelled pistols, "two vials of refreshment, such as laudanum and strychnine," and, as a disguise, the entire costume of a lady's-maid — no less — dress, bonnet, green veil, and all. Behold him hesitating but one moment, just long enough to write upon the unfinished score of the Ball Scene in his "Symphonie Fantastique" directions as to how, if the work is played "in his absence," the flute part may be doubled with the clarinets and horns. Behold him, after this lucid interval, travelling to Genoa, where he either attempts suicide by drowning or falls into the water and is fished out by bystanders — his account is somewhat ambiguous — and where he buys a second lady's-maid's costume, having absent-mindedly left the first one in the coach. And then, with his arrival at Nice, he feels that he has done his duty by the part of the wronged lover, he feels that it would be a pity to deprive the world of his still unwritten compositions; youth pleads the charm of life, the beauty of the Italian landscape, and prudence suggests a brief note to the director of the Academy at Rome, providing for a possible return to the fold. "I stop in Nice a whole month, wandering through the orange groves, diving in the sea, sleeping on the mountain heaths. . . . I live wholly alone, and write the overture to 'King Lear.' I sing, I believe in God. Convalescence has set in." "It is thus," he ingenuously concludes his account of this episode, "that I passed in Nice the twenty happiest days of my life."

On returning to Paris, in 1832, and finding Miss Smithson again playing there, Berlioz tried again, and this time with success, the device of giving a concert of his own works. His "Symphonie Fantastique" and its sequel "Lelio," a monodrama with recitation, were given entire. Whatever might be her ignorance of music, Miss Smithson could hardly fail to divine the reference to herself of a typical passage in the text of "Lelio": "O that I could find her, the *Juliet*, the *Ophelia*, that my heart calls to. That I could drink in the intoxication of that mingled joy and sadness that only true love knows! Could I but rest in her arms one autumn evening, rocked by the north wind on some wild heath, and sleep my last, sad sleep!" This somewhat florid wooing was effective; on the day after the concert the oddly assorted pair met for the first time, and in the following summer were married. In taking this daring step Berlioz seems for once to have manfully forgotten his audience and his dramatic unities, and to have acted quite simply and from the heart. His Ophelia was no longer a favorite of the public; she was now neglected and deeply in debt; she had had the misfortune to break her leg in stepping from her carriage, an accident which threatened to end her career on the stage; her parents, as well as his own, were bitterly opposed to the match. In spite of all, Berlioz married her, and made no literary material out of the event except to weave about it one of his incisive antitheses: "On the day of our wedding she had nothing but debts; I, for my part, had three hundred francs . . . and had quarrelled again with my parents. But she was mine, I bade defiance to everything." It is much to his credit, too, that when his wife was ill, he quite simply set aside a symphony at which he was working, and wrote feuilletons in order to make more money for her.

But the one thing to which Berlioz could

never effectually bid defiance was the radical inconstancy of his own temperament. Once captured and domesticated, his Ophelia began to prove dull; the part of husband gave little play to his romantic capacities; and when he took less and less pains to disguise his boredom, she became jealous even to shrewishness. Presently he sought distraction in the least creditable of all his amours. If the Smithson affair had been drama, or at the least melodrama, and the Mooke episode harmless comedy, the liaison with Mademoiselle Recio, aside from its tragic results, was broad farce. This lady was a second-rate vocalist with an insatiable ambition to sing Berlioz's works, in order to defeat which he had often to resort to ignominious flight, covered by petty prevarication. His devotion to her cannot have resulted in much happiness, and it entirely alienated him from his wife, from whom he separated about 1840. Nevertheless, when she died in 1854, he promptly married this Mademoiselle Recio, with whom he lived in uneasy partnership for eight years.

One of the strangest instances of his morbid appetite for effect at any cost, of the habit of posturing and parading his emotions which ruled him even in matters which should be most private and sacred, is the passage in the autobiography in which he describes, with a Poe-like zest for revolting detail, the reburial of his first wife beside the second in the cemetery of Mont-Martre. The incredible passage need not be quoted in detail, but ends with this sentence, in which the egotism of the sentimentalist stands as naked as it is unashamed: "The two departed ones rest here in peace [*sic*] to this hour, awaiting the time when I shall bring my own portion of rottenness to that charnel-house." This is an extreme instance of the posturing, the attitudinizing, the grandiloquence and rhetoric, to which Berlioz is always tempted more or less in his accounts of his personal doings and feelings. He does not wilfully misrepresent, but he balks at the grayness of mere fact; he is not exactly a liar, but his romantic imagination simply cannot envisage the commonplace; involuntarily he suppresses here, distorts or exaggerates there, in order that his story may have the spectacular vividness, the dramatic éclat, which alone can satisfy him.

On the other hand, whenever, treating of general topics, as he does in the "Soirées d' Orchestre," the "A Travers Chants," and the "Grotesques de la Musique," he can avoid the pitfall of the confidential, he is one of the most charming of writers. Here his instinct for the salient leads him to put everything in the most vivid, captivating way, but without perversion; one no longer has the uncomfortable sense of being hoaxed, and can give oneself up to the enjoyment of his rich play of metaphor and allusion, his subtle irony, his unfailing good-nature, and his nervous, incisive style. Here, in short, his extraordinary intellectual vivacity is revealed at its best, undegraded by being made to serve those posings which, if not precisely dishonest, are still not quite ingenuous. His description, for example, of the machinations of the *claqueurs* or hired applauders at the opera house, known in Parisian slang as "Romans," in the seventh and eighth evenings of the "Soirées d' Orchestre," [1] deserves a niche of its own in the literature of satire. After

---

[1] See " Selections from Berlioz's Writings," translated by W. F. Apthorp, New York, 1879, pp. 228–261.

writing at some length "de viris illustribus urbis Romae," he goes on to enumerate the amateurs who swell the ranks of the *claque*, as follows: —

"They are: simple friends, who admire in good faith all that is to be done on the stage before the lamps are lighted; relations, those *claqueurs* given by nature; editors, ferocious *claqueurs;* and especially lovers and husbands. That is why women, besides the host of other advantages they have over men, have still one more chance of success than they. For a woman can hardly applaud her husband or lover to any purpose in a theatre or concert room; besides, she always has something else to do; while the husband or lover, provided he has the least natural capacity or some elementary notions of the art, can often bring about a success of renewal at the theatre. . . . Husbands are better than lovers for this sort of operation. The latter usually stand in fear of ridicule; they also fear *in petto* that a too brilliant success may make too many rivals; they no longer have any pecuniary interest in the triumphs of their mistresses. But the husband, who holds the purse-strings, who knows

what can be done by a well-thrown bouquet, a
well taken-up salvo, a well-communicated
emotion, a well-carried recall, he alone dares
to turn to account what faculties he has. He
has the gift of ventriloquism and of ubiquity.
He applauds for an instant from the amphi-
theatre, crying out: *Brava!* in a tenor voice,
in chest tones; thence he flies to the lobby of
the first boxes, and sticking his head through
the opening cut in the door, he throws out an
Admirable! in a voice of *basso profundo* while
passing by, and then bounds breathless up to
the third tier, from whence he makes the house
resound with exclamations: 'Delicious! ravish-
ing! Heavens! what talent! it is too much!'
in a *soprano* voice, in shrill feminine tones
stifled with emotion. There is a model husband for you, and a hard-working and intelligent father of a family."

The impression of paradox so markedly given
by Berlioz's prose writings, in which such insight, wit, and good humor as we have here
coexist with the tendency to pose revealed in
his accounts of his love affairs, is intensified by
his musical compositions. In them also he

seems actuated by a desire, not to communicate his real feelings in their simplicity, but to project them into a dramatic conception, and to present that with all the pomp and circumstance of which he is capable. Not truth to inner experience, but vividness of external effect, is his ideal. Yet to the service of this ideal he brings admirable intellectual qualities: ingenuity, resourcefulness, imagination, an originality that scorns all platitude, and, at least in the matter of instrumentation, a matchless technical skill. The brilliant performance of rather specious undertakings — that is Berlioz's artistic cue.

This combination of trivial ends with highly clever means may be illustrated by the "Symphonie Fantastique," a work which, though written early in his career, remains one of his most characteristic productions. How different, to begin with, are the inspirations which a romanticist and a realist derive from the passion of love! Schumann, married to Clara Wieck after years of waiting, utters his joy in a series of songs, the most lyrical, the most intimate, that song literature has to show. Chopin, in an amorous revery, writes in the larghetto of the F-minor Concerto one of the quietest, simplest, most devout of all his pieces. Berlioz, on the contrary, is goaded by the thought of his Ophelia to conceive "a young musician of unhealthily sensitive nature," who "has poisoned himself with opium in a paroxysm of love-sick despair," and to carry this hero through a very detailed drama in five acts.[1] His impulse is, in short, realistic rather than lyrical, and the art in which he embodies it is descriptive and narrative rather than emotionally expressive.

The most important technical result of this realistic attitude is that Berlioz, as we have already noted, treats his melodies, not as materials for a purely musical development, but as symbols of characters or other dramatic motives, thereby anticipating the *leit-motif* idea which later became so prominent in the work of Wagner and Liszt. The central motive in the "Symphonie Fantastique" is the melody known as "*l'idée fixe*," symbolizing the beloved, roughly transcribed for the piano in Figure XXIV.

[1] See the summary of the program of the "Symphonie Fantastique" at p. 24.

Figure XXIV.
Allegro agitato.
1st V. and Flute.

This melody, though it appears in each of the
five movements, undergoes but little evolution;
it is complete in the first place, and in its later
phases is often modified hardly at all, or if so
chiefly for dramatic reasons. In the Ball Scene
two phrases of it are sounded pianissimo, by
the clarinet, just after a sounding climax of

the full orchestra,[1] to indicate the hero's remembrance of the beloved in the midst of the festivities. In the third movement, "In the Country," it is given to the oboe and flute (full score, p. 66), and is treated somewhat more ingeniously, its fifth phrase being interrupted by a rough tumult in all the strings. In "The Procession to the Stake" it figures purely as a theatrical property in a highly characteristic and amusing passage. The hero has finished his long march to the place of execution; as he puts his head on the block silence descends upon the scene, and then a single clarinet plays four measures of the theme — "Ah! he thinks of her once more" — but the thought is cut short by a blow of the axe (fortissimo chord, *tutti*) and the death-rattle (tremolando on three kettle-drums) ends the movement and his life together. Only in the last movement, the frenetic "Witches' Sabbath," is the theme really varied. Here, at p. 102, it appears as in Figure XXV, turned by change of rhythm and the addition of ornament into a grotesque, undignified dance tune.

[1] Full score, Breitkopf and Härtel edition, p. 54.

Figure XXV.

This is certainly clever, but the incentive, we must remember, is still dramatic rather than musical — it is intended to show the loved one degraded to the horrid form of a witch.

There are many other subordinate features of the technique in which may be discerned the same preoccupation with spectacular effect rather than with musical beauty. The mere noise resorted to by the composer in tuning his drums in the third movement, in order to imitate thunder, has already been mentioned;[1] there is a deal of even more chaotic pandemonium in the last two movements. When the harmonies are in themselves consonant, they are sometimes combined so incongruously as to

[1] See Introduction, p. 43.

obliterate all sense of tonality and to generate merely a feeling of haste and confusion, as at page 94 in the score, where the chords of D-flat-major and G-minor tread on one another's heels; so unprecedented was this association of remote harmonies that Berlioz thought it necessary to point out in a foot-note that it was no clerical error, and to beg the violins and violas not to "correct" their parts. Even the scholastic and highly formal device of the fugato he treats with the *sang froid* of the habitual impressionist in that weird section of the "Witches' Sabbath" in which he makes a sort of devil's fugue, lost in limbo, on the rhythm of the witches' round dance (score, p. 132).

Yet how remarkable is the skill with which he works out his so perverse ideal! His melodies, however they may lack lyrical quality, are always of definite contour and arresting individuality, and frequently of an odd half-insidious, half-challenging appeal. Though Mr. Hadow's charge that "time after time he ruins his cause by subordinating beauty to emphasis, and is so anxious to impress that he forgets how to charm" is undoubtedly just, yet equally true is his further remark that "his sense of rhythm was, at the time when he lived, without parallel in the history of music." Thanks to this sense of rhythm he entirely avoided those wall-paper patterns which make much of the music of romanticism so formally monotonous, and he attained often a splendidly complex, though generally slightly mechanical, organization of phrases. The *idée fixe* is a good example of this prosodic elasticity. It consists of an eight-measure phrase balanced by one of seven measures, four phrases of four measures each in climactic sequence, and a codetta made up of a pair of two-measure phrases and a final phrase of five measures; and with all this variety, the unity of the tune as a whole is unimpeachable. The melody of the song "La Captive" (see Figure XXVI) is most fascinating in its irregular regularity, in the perfect

Figure XXVI.

naturalness with which three-measure and two-measure groups alternate and intertwine. In fact, Berlioz is a master of what in poetry we call versification.

His skill in orchestration is notorious. "Berlioz claims attention first and foremost," says one critic, "as a master of orchestration, perhaps the most ingenious and versatile among all modern composers"; [1] and another ranks him with Beethoven, Wagner, and Dvořák as "one of the four greatest masters of instrumentation the world has ever seen." [2] Unfortunately even in this department he could not entirely resist that craving for sensationalism which was the characteristic vice of his temperament; so that his name has become associated in many minds with merely noisy or eccentric effects

[1] E. Dickinson, "The Study of the History of Music," p. 264.

[2] W. H. Hadow, "Studies in Modern Music," p. 141.

that are far from representing him at his best. He loved to pile Pelion upon Ossa, scored his Requiem for sixteen trombones, sixteen trumpets, five ophicleides, twelve horns, eight pairs of kettle-drums, two bass drums, and a gong, in addition to the usual resources, and told with pride of its having frightened one of the listeners into a fit. He was frequently rallied for what Mr. Nordau would call his "megalomania." "Prince Metternich," he tells us in his memoirs, "said to me one day: 'Are you not the man, monsieur, who composes music for five hundred performers?' To which I replied: 'Not always, monseigneur; I sometimes write for four hundred and fifty.'"

Love of the bizarre and the unusual led him often to employ rare instruments, or to use the ordinary ones in freakish ways. The harp, the English horn, and the cornet figure frequently in his scores, and he likes to direct that the horns be put in bags, that the cymbal be suspended and struck with a stick, that the drums be played with sticks covered with sponge. In one instance he ventures a duet between a piccolo and a bass trombone. He describes, in a letter from Germany, a trick by which a trombone player sounds four tones at once, and adds in all seriousness: "Acousticians ought to explain this new phenomenon in the resonance of sonorous tubes; we musicians ought to study it thoroughly and turn it to account when the opportunity presents itself." He was one of the earliest and most indefatigable champions of the valve horns and trumpets made by Sax of Paris, and also, by a less happy inspiration, made propaganda for the *cornet à pistons*, which is in comparison with its noble cousin, the trumpet, a most vulgar instrument. He was a daring, but not always a cautious, innovator, frequently seeming to set a higher value upon novelty than upon inherent worth.

His real claim to distinction as a master of the orchestra, however, rests not upon his extravagances, but upon his wonderfully delicate, unerring instinct for the capacities of the common instruments for tone color, both alone and in combination. It has been well said of him that he "thought orchestrally," that with him "the tone color was an essential part of the original design." The themes of the "Dance

of Sprites" and the "Dance of Sylphs," in the
"Damnation of Faust" (see Figure XXVII),

Figure XXVII.

are not merely "tunes," in the generic sense of
the word, adaptable to any medium; the first
is distinctively a piccolo tune, the second a
violin melody. This instinctive sense of what

each member of the orchestral family can best
do gives Berlioz's sound-mass an unrivalled
clarity, felicity, and distinction; it enables him
to solve every problem that arises in a quite unconventional way, proceeding, without regard
to tradition, to the precise timbre he has imagined, with the economy and certainty of a
master. His scores are apt to look rather
empty, because he allows so many instruments
to remain silent; but they do not sound empty,
for each tone is placed where it will "tell" to
the utmost, yet without blurring any other.
The two dances just mentioned are models of
this kind of discretion, as also is the Ball Scene
in the "Symphonie Fantastique," in which the
variety of the combinations obtained from a
few instruments is surprising. First the violins
alone play the tune, accompanied by the other
strings (page 37 in the full score); then (page
39) the accompaniment is shared between the
strings on the first beat of the measure, two
harps on the second beat, and the wood wind
on the third; next (page 42) second violins,
violas, and 'cellos unite on the melody, the
wood wind and a cornet emphasize the accent,

the first violin embroiders a delicate turn at the end of each measure, and the basses pluck insistent eighth-notes; and finally all the wood wind and the harps take up the tune (at page 47) to an accompaniment of horns and harps. The marvel of it is that all these tonal schemes are of such a perfect elasticity, such a brilliant lightness; this is musical champagne, that makes most other scores seem vapid and heavy, like wine too long uncorked.

The same intellectual ingenuity, curiously dissociated from emotional earnestness, which made Berlioz so clever a melodist and so inimitable a master of orchestral effects, enabled him also to achieve those innovations in the general scheme and intention of instrumental music on which his historical importance mainly depends. By discerning that, although the principle of coherence in all classical and lyrico-romantic music was the interplay and logical evolution of melodies or themes, that is, of purely musical elements, yet a composition might be unified rather by the interplay of characters and events, or in other words of dramatic motives, of which the music was merely representative, he opened the way for Liszt and the modern program composers. He thus became the pioneer of that realistic movement which in our own day has assumed such prominence, providing, as early as 1830, in the "Symphonie Fantastique," which is essentially a realistic work, with program and leading motives, the prototype of many famous modern masterpieces.

The most striking, and to us nowadays the most familiar, of all applications of this scheme of dramatic form is of course that of Wagner in his music-dramas. So far as Wagner's art was conscious it was planned entirely from the dramatic point of view. In the matter of tune he laid stress on "emotive expression," to borrow once more M. Goblot's term, rather than on symmetry of form, discarding regular phrase-balance and definite metre in favor of a loosely knit recitative, quickly responsive to all changes of mood, which he called "infinite melody." So far as definite musical figures appeared at all, they were conceived, not as having any intrinsic value, but as standing for extra-musical ideas: that is, they were not "subjects" or "themes," they were "leading-motives." The larger forms underwent a similar modification; the Italian aria, consisting of a melody, a second contrasting melody, and a repetition of the first, was discarded, in spite of its architectonic beauty, as being undramatic, since action never repeats itself, but ceaselessly changes. Even in purely instrumental pieces the principle of coherence became the imitation of a natural series of events or ideas. One looks in vain, in the "Funeral March" in "Götterdämmerung," for the kind of thematic development which makes so splendidly organic the "Funeral March" of Beethoven's "Eroica Symphony"; the unity of Wagner's piece depends on its being the narration of the events in the life of a single hero, Siegfried. The Prelude to "Lohengrin," though incidentally a masterpiece of purely musical structure, was conceived as a tone-picture of the descent from heaven, and the return thither, of an angel host bearing the Holy Grail. A more extreme case is the Prelude to the "Rheingold," in which there is no musical structure at all, the whole piece being written upon one unchanging harmony; the motive there is entirely pictorial. Finally, the descriptive and imitative elements in expression are prominent in such characteristic Wagnerian passages as the fire-music and the "Waldweben."

Wagner has thus become the standard instance of a musician dominated by a dramatic ideal, and has proved conclusively the powers of music associated with action. But this "music associated with action," it must be noted, is not, strictly speaking, any longer music at all, but a new art, to which its creator gave the name of music-drama: it appeals not only to the ear through sounds, but to the eye through scenery and actors, and to the understanding through language. To apply the principles which naturally dominate so composite an art as this to the writing of pure instrumental music is a daring and a questionable innovation, which we owe to Berlioz and Liszt. It is one thing to compose in this style a work to be played, sung, and acted in an opera-house, and quite another to cut from the same stuff a symphony to be performed by staid musicians in conventional dress in the concert-room. That Wagner himself was well aware of the difference is shown by a passage in his essay on Liszt's Symphonic Poems, striking enough to be quoted at some length.

"I pardon everybody," says the great music-dramatist, "who has doubted the benefit of a new art-form for instrumental music, for I must own to having so fully shared that doubt as to join those who saw in our program-music a most unedifying spectacle — whereby I felt the drollness of my situation, as I myself was classed among just the program-musi-cians, and cast into one pot with them. Whilst listening to the best of this sort . . . it had always happened that I so completely lost the musical thread that by no manner of exertion could I re-find and knit it up again. This occurred to me quite recently with the love-scene, so entrancing in its principal motives, of our friend Berlioz's 'Romeo and Juliet Sym-phony'; the great fascination which had come over me during the development of the chief motive was dispelled in the further course of the movement, and sobered down to an un-deniable *malaise;* I discovered at once that, while I had lost the musical thread (*i.e.* the logical and lucid play of definite motives), I now had to hold on to scenic motives not present before my eye, nor even so much as ,indicated in the program. . . . The musician looks quite away from the incidents of ordinary life, entirely upheaves its details and its accidents, and sublimates whatever lies within it to its quintessence of emotional content — to which alone can music give a voice, and music only. A true musical poet, therefore, would have presented Berlioz with this scene in a thoroughly compact *ideal* form."

Wagner here puts his finger on the chief points of weakness in Berlioz's ingenious scheme. The lack of what he calls the musical thread, and defines most concisely as "the logical and lucid play of definite motives," is indeed a most serious defect, as we have already seen in the case of the "Symphonie Fantastique." Because of it, the composer's best effects seem fragmentary and uncoördinated; however we enjoy his brilliant, affecting, or powerful moments, we miss the sense of inexorable progress, of deliberate accumulation of force, of efflorescence of melodic germs as slow and as steady as a process of nature, which is so overwhelming in the music of Bach and Beethoven. His music is almost always interesting rather than beautiful; he lets our attention dissipate itself upon picturesque details, instead of seizing and concentrating it by the grandeur of his design, the symmetry of his forms, the logic of their evolution. His structures, considered as wholes, however massive and imposing, are fundamentally incoherent; his rhythms, for all their ingenuity, are over-whimsical, restless; his harmony is often awkward, strained, non-sequacious. He cares less for purity than for pungency of style, and seems to be entirely unconscious of the large alloy of incongruity and anticlimax that adulterates his finest conceptions.

These shortcomings were by no means accidental; their cause lay deep in his peculiar temperament. "Berlioz's disposition," says one of his critics with penetration,[1] "was instinctively somewhat inclined to the grotesque; he had

[1] Francis Hueffer, "Half a Century of Music in England," pp. 231–232.

not that inborn reverence for the proprieties of nature which is the secret of the highest art achievement. He set his individuality . . . above immutable law." Indeed, Berlioz had more than the usual share of the romanticist's indifference to abstract beauty in art, and of the romanticist's impatience of the discipline which alone gives command of it. When he was a boy he showed on every occasion his "unquestioning intolerance of prescriptive right"; he dismissed Lesueur's harmony as "antediluvian," and Reicha's counterpoint as "barbarous." When he was a man he frankly expressed his boredom at the most perfect of musical forms: "A theme without a fugue," he writes in, one of his letters, "is rare good luck"; in another he exclaims, "May God preserve you from fugues with four themes on a choral!"; and his attitude towards Bach, the touchstone of all musical taste, is in strange contrast with that of Schumann, Mendelssohn, Chopin, and indeed almost all of his great contemporaries. "When I was in St. Petersburg," he tells us, "they played me a triple concerto of Bach's. . . . I do not think they intended to

annoy me." In the light of such a confession
we are not surprised to find him, in the famous
passage in the autobiography wherein he sets
forth his pretensions as a composer, making no
claim to the highest qualities, to grandeur, restraint, poise, proportion, beauty, but content-
ing himself with the words, "The dominant
qualities of my music are passionate expression, internal fire, rhythmic animation, and unexpected changes."

On the other hand, if he was in some degree
forced into the dramatic vein by deficiencies on
the musical side, he had also some strong positive qualifications for the work he undertook.
A degree of literary cultivation rare among
musicians gave him a large choice of motives
to draw upon. The symphony, "Romeo and
Juliet," the overture, "King Lear," the opera,
"Beatrice and Benedict," the "Tempest"
fantasia in "Lelio," and some minor pieces,
all owe their inspiration to Shakspere; Byron
is drawn upon for the "Corsair" overture and
the symphony, "Harold in Italy," and Scott for
the overtures, "Waverley" and "Rob Roy";
Goethe for "The Damnation of Faust"; the

autobiography of Benvenuto Cellini for the overture which bears his name, and Virgil's "Æneid" for the opera, "The Trojans at Carthage." It is true that both in his choice and his utilization of texts he was often characteristically perverse. He considered Thomas Moore one of the great pathetic poets of the world; he garbled "Romeo and Juliet"; he placed Faust in Hungary in order to introduce the Racokzy March; he made the demons in "Faust" sing in Swedenborg's infernal language — "*Irimiru Karabrao! Has! Has! Tradioun Marexil firtrudinxé burrudixé*" . . .; in his own programs he perpetrated, with entire gravity, the most mirth-provoking medleys of the sublime and the ridiculous. Yet in spite of his lack of humor, and even at times of ordinary common sense, he brought to the planning and execution of his fantastic conceptions an extraordinary cleverness.

Berlioz is, however, even as a dramatist, open to severe criticism, the nature of which is again suggested by Wagner. In pointing out that in the absence of a purely musical thread one has to hold on to "scenic motives not present to the eye, nor even so much as indicated in the program," Wagner touches upon one of the ineradicable defects of all program-music, its ambiguity. Doubtless it is quite possible, and mildly amusing, to follow, on hearing the "Symphonie Fantastique," the general outlines of the story, but did Berlioz suppose that any one would be able to recognize in his music, otherwise often unintelligible, the details of the "plot"? If so, he was certainly overrating the descriptive powers of sound, and placing too much dependence on the definiteness of a medium which is by nature vague and indeterminate. He was himself conscious of the difficulty; but with his usual arrogance he attributed it, not to any shortcoming in his own art, but to his audience's lack of imagination. To the sixth division of the score of "Romeo and Juliet" he appends this foot-note: "The public has no imagination; pieces which address themselves solely to the imagination have consequently no public. The following instrumental scene is in this predicament, and I think it should be suppressed except when the symphony is to be heard by an audience of the élite, to whom the fifth act of Shakspere's tragedy, with Garrick's dénoûement, is extremely familiar, and whose poetic sentiment is very elevated." The thought that possibly a piece of music should not address itself solely to the pictorial imagination does not seem to have occurred to him.

When Berlioz's music does not fail of its effect through being ambiguous, it is very apt to lose itself in triviality; indeed, this, as we have already seen,[1] is one of the imminent dangers besetting all program-music. Why is it that we are rather more inclined to smile than to shudder at the piled-up horrors of the "Witches' Sabbath"? Why does the elaborate machinery which Berlioz assembles in order to stun us leave us so often rather amused or bored? Why is it that we enjoy more than we resent that parody of his style perpetrated by Arnal, in which we are asked "to understand from the second repetition of the first allegro how my hero ties his cravat"? Is it not that there is involved in the programmistic method a subtle insult to our intelligence, that

[1] Introduction, p. 53.

we instinctively rebel against the use of musical tones, by nature so uniquely expressive of inner verities, for the mere delineation of external objects? Wagner seems to think so when, in the last part of his criticism, he says that the musician "looks quite away from the incidents of ordinary life . . . and sublimates whatever lies within it to its quintessence of emotional-content." Bourget certainly thinks so when he commands the artist, "*Sois belle et tais-toi.*"

This highest simplicity of the great creative artist, who ignores the accidents and the externals of life, who "looks into his heart and writes," was just what Berlioz, with all his mobile intelligence, all his ingenuity, all his earnest aspiration, could never achieve. There was in him a perversity of temper, a disharmony between the emotional and the intellectual nature, a lack of the sense of proportion or the sense of humor, which made it impossible. The natural seemed to him jejune; the simple, vulgar; the impulsive, crude. To be elaborate, theatrical, calculated, was a necessity of his highly artificial imagination. Just as in his love affairs he was never following an unsophisticated passion, but forever masquerading as an ideal hero, and as in his essays and autobiography he never chronicled, but always dramatized, so in his compositions he could not bring himself to express spontaneous intuitions in naïve forms, but built up elaborate programs with all the ingenuity of his tireless and resourceful intelligence. All life appeared to him as a magnificent glittering spectacle in which he was playing a leading rôle; and whether he loved or hated, whether he suffered or enjoyed, whether he succeeded or failed, he hugged close to his Gallic heart the consciousness that he was acting well, and that he had an audience. Like the firemen of Beauvais, he had, too, the ineffable satisfaction of placarding the heavens, in his autobiography, with the inspiring legend, "Honneur aux victimes du devoir."

The boast in his case, nevertheless, was far from an empty one; not the least strange element in his strangely mixed character was the real heroism, the splendid faith, with which he clung to an artistic ideal which was received with contempt or indifference on every side.

In his devotion to an unpopular cause, through a lifetime of difficulties, he was a true martyr. His career, after his return from Rome to Paris in 1832, was one long uphill fight, not only for recognition, but for a bare livelihood. His accounts of his hated labors as a feuilletonist, up to the time when, by a generous gift from Paganini, he was freed from such servitude, are among the sincerest and most pathetic pages in his writings. He never won the appreciation from his countrymen that his vain, sensitive, and thoroughly Parisian nature most craved. Realizing, about 1840, that a man is never a prophet in his own country, he reluctantly sought abroad the support denied him at home, and in a series of tours in Germany, Austria, Russia, and England met with a large measure of success. Yet his first care, after each foreign triumph, was to know "what they thought of it in Paris" — and alas! they never thought about it at all. Tardily, in 1856, already over fifty years old, he obtained a *fauteuil* in the Academy, and was appointed Librarian of the Conservatoire. But the cheering effect of this recognition was clouded by the fiasco, in 1863, of the opera on which he had been working for years, "Les Troyens à Carthage." This blow broke his heart. He wrote no more, and after six years of loneliness and ill-health, died on March 8, 1869. As so often happens, his funeral orations contained the enthusiastic praises his living ears had craved in vain, and he was shortly pronounced the greatest of French composers.

The faith in himself and his art, which kept him steadfast through all his discouragements and temptations, which enabled him to persist in a path of almost complete solitude, which armed him with the sword of conviction and the shield of a good conscience, was, as Mr. Apthorp says, "the one pure, sterling element in a character in which all else was more or less distorted." He was a man of overweening vanity and egotism, often blind to the needs of those nearest him; an uncertain friend, a spiteful enemy, an intolerable husband; he could descend to petty deceits and unworthy animosities, and was willing to sacrifice the most sacred relations on the altar of his dramatic sense. And yet he could say with truth, "The love of money has never allied itself in a single instance with my love of art; I have always been ready to make all sorts of sacrifices to go in search of the beautiful, and insure myself against contact with those paltry platitudes which are crowned by popularity." He had also many minor virtues which, if not like this precisely heroic, are nevertheless charming. He was a sprightly narrator, a witty and keen critic where his prejudices were not involved, and a taster of life in whom discrimination did not embitter good nature.

Concerning his achievement as a musician there will always be extreme oppositions of opinion, so uncompromising was his theory of art, and so relentless his execution of it. The ultimate problem of whether a realism so thoroughgoing as his is justified by the nature of music will perhaps always remain an open one. But the most recalcitrant critic must admit the greatness of his incidental services to the art which he practised with such headlong perversity. He was a good iconoclast. He helped to break the bonds of a narrow conservatism which was in danger of confining all music to the forms of the symphony and the sonata, and to the type of expression perfected by the classicists. By his daring imagination he abashed pedantry and opened up vistas of new possibilities. And he was, at least in one department, that of orchestration, a triumphant innovator. By using instruments, not in traditional, hackneyed ways, but with an intuition of their latent possibilities, he added permanently to the resources of all composers and to the sensitiveness of all listeners. Whether, therefore, the tendency of all music toward the realistic, which is so prominent to-day, and in relation to which he stands as one of the greatest of pioneers, shall continue indefinitely, or shall give place to some new movement in another direction, as certain signs seem to indicate — in any event Berlioz's place as a contributor to the unresting progress of art is secure.

VII

FRANZ LISZT

—

FRANZ LISZT

FRANZ LISZT

—

A FLOOD of light is thrown upon the opposing aspects of Franz Liszt's contradictory character by a story told of a certain occasion on which "The Master," as he loved to be called, sat for his portrait to the painter Schaffer. One of those key-stories it is, dear to biographers, which condense in single acts or speeches entire facets of personality. In Paris, in his youth, Liszt went to Schaffer to have his portrait painted. Instinctively he assumed one of those theatrical poses he was in the habit of taking when, at the end of one of his already famous recitals, he stood upon the stage receiving the plaudits of his audience. We can readily imagine it: the head thrown back, the eyes flashing fire, the right hand, perhaps, thrust between the second and third buttons of the coat, the left resting on some conveniently composed piece of furniture. But when Schaffer indicated that this histrionism did not impress him, Liszt, greatly embarrassed, cried out impulsively, "Forgive, dear master, but you do not know how it spoils one to have been an infant prodigy." Here are the two opposing sides of this curious character for once set in a clear antithesis: on the one hand, the affectation, the strut and posture, the cheap theatricality, of the prodigy playing to his audience; on the other, the frankness, the magnanimity, the humility even, of the true artist. Liszt's whole career is one long exhibition of these two attitudes in constant alternation; he is a mingling in one person of the charlatan and the idealist.

Born in Raiding, a small town in Hungary, October 22, 1811, an only child of Adam Liszt, a Hungarian, and Anna Lager, a German, Franz Liszt showed at once such extraordinary talent for music that in his tenth year his parents resolved to educate him in Vienna as a professional musician. After a year and a half in the Austrian capital, where the brilliancy of his piano playing and the cleverness of his improvisations attracted much attention, and where he studied with Czerny and Salieri, he was taken by his parents to Paris. Here, in the autumn of 1823, only twelve years old, he took his first plunge into the atmosphere of adulation which was to become to him in later years almost a necessary of life. It was now that he became the petted darling of the fashionable salons of the Boulevard St. Germain, and made the great ladies of Parisian society forget for a time their lap-dogs and their love-intrigues in order to caress this fascinating composite of the child and the virtuoso. After his first public concert in Paris, in March, 1824, he "made the round of the boxes," a sort of triumphal progress across the laps of great ladies, who wooed him, we must suppose, with a discreet mixture of compliments and bonbons. In the following spring he extended his dominion to England, and saw his name in large type on a hand-bill such as nowadays we associate with circuses rather than with concerts. "An Air," we read, "with Grand Variations by Herz, will be performed on Erard's New Patent Grand Pianoforte, by

MASTER LISZT,

who will likewise perform an Extempore Fantasia, and respectfully request *Two Written Themes* from any of the Audience, upon which he will play his Variations."

There are not wanting signs, however, that the artist in Liszt was already, with approaching adolescence, beginning to disdain the spectacular triumphs of the virtuoso. He began to suspect that "the praise belongs to the child and not the artist"; the indignity of being advertised as a year or two younger than he really was, and being carried upon the stage in his manager's arms, like an infant, aroused his disgust; "I would rather be anything in the world," he cries, "than a musician in the pay of great folk, patronized and paid by them like a conjurer or the clever dog Munito."[1] He became more and more reluctant to appear in public, grew moody and melancholy, occupied himself with religious meditations, and even cherished a half-formed desire to withdraw from the brilliant world into monastic solitude.

[1] Ramann, "Life of Liszt," Eng. trans., I, 218.

This is the first appearance of a mystical
tendency of mind which in later years gained
great ascendancy over him, and finally led him
to take orders in the Roman Catholic Church.
The event, however, which decisively ended,
for the time, his public piano playing, was the
death, in August, 1827, of his father, whose
assistance in all practical details was indispensable to his virtuoso tours.

The young pianist now settled with his
mother in Paris, where eight quiet years of
piano teaching succeeded the excitement of his
adventurous boyhood. His conduct at this
crisis illustrates that keen sense of honor which
was so agreeable a trait in his character. Considering that the money he had accumulated by
his many successful concerts was rightfully his
mother's, because of all the sacrifices she had
made to his career, he made it over to her in a
lump sum, and took up teaching for his own
livelihood. It was an act of delicate justice,
freely and cheerfully performed. Outwardly
Liszt's life now became quite simple and
laborious, almost plodding; but inwardly it
was developing apace, and ramifying in many

directions, under the provocations of this brilliant and complex Paris.

The Paris of 1830 was indeed a surrounding well fitted to encourage the most varied growth in the character of a young man so sensitive to influences, so complex in mental and moral constitution, as Liszt. There was, on the purely musical side, the powerful irritant of a public languid and frivolous, devoted to the showy tinsel of Kalkbrenner, Herz, Pixis, and Pleyel, and so indifferent to real music that Liszt had to coat the pill of a Beethoven Concerto with sugary ornamentation to make it go down. Such a public was a good stolid quarry for the marksmanship of an enthusiastic artist. In general intellectual life there was, on the other hand, a brisk fermentation highly exciting to Liszt's active mind. Paris was a seething pot of ideas, theories, heresies, aspirations, scepticisms, individualities. "Here is a whole fortnight," he writes in 1832, "that my mind and fingers have been working like two lost spirits — Homer, the Bible, Plato, Locke, Byron, Hugo, Lamartine, Châteaubriand, Beethoven, Bach, Hummel, Mozart, Weber, are all around me.

I study them, meditate on them, devour them with fury; besides this I practise four to five hours of exercises. . . . Ah, provided I don't go mad, you will find an artist in me!" [1] Above all, there was in the French romanticism of 1830 an emotional delirium, a fever of the sentiments, which profoundly affected the high-strung young musician.

French literary romanticism was in essence an extension into the intellectual world of those principles which had received so striking a political embodiment in the French Revolution of 1789. About a generation was required for these principles to propagate themselves from the realm of practice into that of theory; in the Revolution they appeared as crude instincts; romanticism refined and systematized them into self-conscious doctrines. The revolutionary mob murdered the aristocrats who oppressed them; the romanticists proclaimed the effeteness of all arbitrary rules and all traditional ordinances, whether in life or in art. The revolutionists cried, in effect, "Each man for himself, and the devil take the hindmost";

[1] "Letters of Liszt," ed. by La Mara, Eng. trans., I, 8.

the romanticists asserted, more politely but in as anarchic a spirit, "The individual alone is sacred; his development is of greater import than the welfare of society." And if romanticism had its analogue for the "Liberty" of the famous formula in its emancipation from traditional law, and its own version of the "Equality" as the "sacredness of the individual," it also had its equivalent for "Fraternity" in that somewhat hectic sentiment which usually proved too vaporous to bear the stress of an actual human situation. Both movements, too, were passionate exaggerations; they overshot their mark, and have had to be limited, qualified, and restrained by the saner sense of later generations.

If romanticism had everywhere this general character of revolt against authority, assertion of the individual, and deification of the sentiments, it is notable that while in England it applied its theories chiefly to political and religious life, and in Germany to metaphysical realms, in France it concentrated itself largely upon the relations of the sexes. In such typical romantic documents as Châteaubriand's "René"

and George Sand's "Leone Leoni," the traditional bugaboo is marriage (especially the
mariage de convenance, which indeed was a fair
mark for reformers), the extolled individualism
takes the form of free love, and the sentiments
deified are the thrills of the amorous heart.
The results of the over-enthusiastic application
of these romantic ideas to so complex a matter
as sexual relations are sometimes bewildering,
sometimes absurd, sometimes pathetic. George
Sand's utterances on love and friendship, for
example, often leave one uncertain whether to
laugh or to cry, so generous is her primary impulse, so sophistical and topsy-turvy are the
conclusions to which it opens the way. When
she writes, "The greater the crime, so much
the more genuine the love it accomplishes," our
anger at the sophism quickly gives place to
pity for the sophist. When we learn that her
ideal of friendship between a man and a woman,
or, as she called it, *camaraderie*, involved "un-
limited confidential conversations," we know
not which to doubt, her insight or her good
faith. And in all this she is typical of her
age and school, which made a fetich of the

"demoniac power of love," and pursued liaisons with a fervor that can only be called religious.

The effect of such doctrines as these on a young man like Liszt may readily be imagined. Too keen-minded to be really deceived by the current fallacies, but at the same time not austere or independent enough to reject what was so universally accepted, he let himself go with the current, and half-blindly, half-ironically, played the game he saw others playing. Almost before he knew it he found that he had staked nothing less than his honor, and that this game, begun in a mood of dalliance, must be played through in sober earnest. The heroine of his love affair was the Countess d'Agoult, better known by her literary pseudonym of Daniel Stern, a woman of great beauty and fascination, but apparently consumed by vanity and a thirst for power. In 1834, when her connection with the idolized young musician began, she was twenty-eight years old, had been married for six years to the Count d'Agoult, and had had three children. In the following spring, Liszt tried in vain to bring the affair to an end;

finding this impossible, he accepted the situation with the best grace he could summon, and entered upon a period of travel with the countess which lasted a decade. Three children resulted from this union, Daniel, Blandine, and Cosima, who became the wife of Von Bülow, and later of Wagner.

It is difficult to arrive at a just conception of Liszt's behavior in this relation, so conflicting are the available accounts of it. The biography by Ramann, for example, states that he offered marriage, which the lady indignantly refused on the score of his inferiority in rank. Janka Wohl, in her "Reminiscences," on the contrary, quotes Liszt's emphatic denial that he ever offered marriage. Again, the very zeal with which his admirers depict the Countess as hurling herself upon him, tend to arouse the suspicion of a judicious reader. One thing is certain, the uncongeniality of the pair was fundamental and cumulative. Liszt himself testifies to this in no uncertain way, and, one may add, with more sarcastic animus than is quite to his credit. He reports a conversation in which she expressed a desire to be his inspirer in art, a desire which he attributes to her vanity. "She wished to be my Beatrice," he says; and continues: "But I told her: 'You are wrong. It is the Dantes who create the Beatrices, and the *real* Beatrices die at the age of eighteen — that is all.' Louis de Ronchaud was present at the time. 'There's the man, said I, 'who would have pleased you.'" This was ungallant almost to the verge of brutality. That verge was overpassed when Liszt, to a request for suggestions as to the title of some souvenirs the countess had been writing, proposed "Swagger and Lies." He always spoke of the countess, says Janka Wohl, with irony.

This picture of a disillusion such as inevitably follows a "grande passion" of the romantic order, unpleasant as it is, helps us to a realization of one side of Liszt, his cynicism. An ironical bitterness such as often lay just below the saccharine smile of this finished man of the world is one of the most familiar byproducts of sentimental romanticism, one which has been made historically famous by the case of Byron. It is the reaction of the enthusiast disappointed in unrealizable ideals, the dreary

320

awakening from overfanciful dreams, the exaggerated contraction of a heart too long artificially expanded, the acidity produced by a
diet all of sugar. It sounds unpleasantly
enough in certain sayings of Liszt quoted by
Janka Wohl: "Women do not believe in a
passion which avoids notoriety." "Misunderstood women are generally women who have
been too well understood." Madame Moscheles
writes, in her reminiscences of Liszt: "His
high-flying notions are made more interesting
by all the arts of dialectics; but there is a good
deal of satire in them, and that satire is like an
ill-tuned chord in conversation. The sugared
charm of his most excellent French cannot
make some of his principles palatable to me."

Closely connected with this cynicism of Liszt
is another marked trait of his character which
at first sight seems to have little connection with
it, but on careful scrutiny is seen to be but
another form of reaction against the sentimental
interpretation of life with its unsocial lawlessness and its self-defeating egotism. That strong
leaning of Liszt's toward the extreme phases of
Roman Catholicism, which made him even in

boyhood a mystic and a devoted reader of
Lamennais, Ballanche, and other ecclesiastical
writers, which impelled him later to take orders,
and which inspired the exclusively devotional
works of his last years, what was it but the
perverse impulse to escape from the world of
a man whom the world has disappointed?
Monasticism is in large part merely the romanticism of the disillusioned. Complete isolation
from human pursuits and feelings is in essence
quite as antisocial, quite as wilfully individual,
as the excesses which carry an exhausted spirit
to its threshold. Liszt's passion for religion,
which has so often puzzled his critics, was in
large degree only the longing for repose of a
soul too long overwrought by the religion of
passion.

It is one of the curiosities of the psychology
of temperament that this new mood of Liszt's,
the mood of mystical passion, found its aspirations crystallizing, no less than those of the
earlier worldly passion had done, in a woman.
If paganism had for a time summed itself for
him in the person of the Countess d'Agoult,
the monastic Christianity to which he now re-

acted found its avatar and priestess in the Princess of Sayn-Wittgenstein, a remarkable woman with whom he lived in intimate but what are called platonic relations from 1847 on. The daughter of a Polish nobleman, and the wife of a Russian field marshal of erratic character whom, after thrice refusing, she married without love at seventeen, she had suffered much, and like many other sufferers had found her consolation in religion. The story of her relation with Liszt is a pathetic one. She deserted her husband to follow him to Weimar, where he settled as a conductor and composer in 1847, after his many years of wandering as a virtuoso; for thirteen years she was his secretary, friend, and adviser; in 1860 she succeeded in getting a divorce from her husband, whose infidelities were notorious, only to have it retracted at the last moment by the Pope. Her spirit was so broken by this cruel freak of fate that, although Prince Wittgenstein died four years later, she never married Liszt. She died in Rome in 1887, only six weeks after Liszt, leaving in manuscript a treatise in twenty-four volumes entitled "Des Causes Intérieures de la

Faiblesse Extérieure de l'Église," with directions
that it should not be printed for twenty-five
years. The subject is one on which she may
well have written with passion; but it is sad
to think of this woman consoling herself, by
twenty-four volumes of literary discussion, for a
vital tragedy.

During the fourteen years that Liszt spent
in Weimar as Music-Director to the Grand
Duke, he accomplished an extraordinary amount
of work, in musical and literary composition,
in teaching, and in making propaganda for
struggling composers by performing their works.
His cordial interest in other artists, perhaps the
finest trait of his character, was at this time
most strikingly evinced. His baton, his pen,
and his powerful personal influence were constantly employed in the service of young musicians of merit striving to make themselves
known. His efforts in Wagner's behalf, especially, have become famous. By his performance of "Lohengrin" at Weimar in 1850,
by his articles on four of the music-dramas, and
by his financial aid to the struggling composer
during many years, he did more than any other

one man to secure this uncompromising genius a foothold in the world. Schumann, Chopin, Berlioz, Raff, Franck, Saint-Saëns, and a host of less gifted men also owed much to Liszt; and his leaving Weimar was the indirect result of his zealous championship of an unpopular opera by his friend Peter Cornelius. It is true that even this benevolence was not quite unalloyed by his besetting egotism. In our mental image of Liszt dispensing his artistic charity there is always a trace of that bland smile of the professional philanthropist. Saint-Saëns suggests that Liszt contemplated, in his relations with Wagner, a sort of alliance of two men of genius, in which Wagner should represent the hero of music-drama, and himself the hero of instrumental music. His rupture with Brahms, who did not appreciate his piano sonata,[1] suggests an inability to forget the first person, excusable perhaps in one so long used to constant adulation, but still not to be neglected in a delineation of his character. Tschaïkowsky's

[1] Brahms is said to have fallen asleep during Liszt's performance of it. See Dr. William Mason's "Memories of a Musical Life."

testimony on the point is very blunt. "Liszt, the old Jesuit," he writes in a letter, "speaks in terms of exaggerated praise of every work which is submitted to his inspection. He is at heart a good man, one of the very few great artists who has never known envy; but he is too much of a Jesuit to be frank and sincere." And again: "Liszt was a good fellow, and ready to respond to every one who paid court to him. But as I never toadied to him, or any other celebrity, we never got into correspondence." But if the great man had thus his petty vanities, if he liked to take a toll of self-satisfaction, so to speak, out of the gifts he so lavished upon others, this human weakness did not, happily, destroy the efficacy of his many services to music.

We have now glanced at three distinct phases in the life of this protean spirit, three rôles successively assumed by him in his triumphal progress across the stage of European society. First there was the infant prodigy, the boy virtuoso, "*le petit Litz*," electrifying vast audiences by his piano playing, and after his concerts "making the round of the boxes." Then

came the slender, romantic youth, Monsieur
Liszt the piano teacher in the Paris of 1830,
with his polished manners, his attractive irony,
his devotion to his mother, and a thousand
suspected gallantries to make him interesting
to the ladies. And then — the third phase —
Liszt without the Monsieur, Liszt of Weimar,
the conductor and propagandist, the composer
of symphonic poems, the prophet of "poetic"
instrumental music, the patron and almoner of
Wagner, the teacher to whom pupils flocked
from all over the world. But now we come to
a fourth phase, stranger, more seizing to the
imagination (especially the feminine imagination) than any of the others: we behold the
former man of the world seated in pious solitude
in the monastery of Monte Mario, near Rome,
his personable figure swathed in the long black
robe of an ecclesiastical order, his ingratiating
smile touched with a celestial joy, his throng-
ing thoughts transferred from Paris to Paradise.
Here he sits, in rapt devotion, for seven years.
He has thrown aside the secular pen, and writes
only masses and oratorios. He has become, in
two words, the Abbé Liszt.

From his retirement, however, he again reappears in the arena of his early triumphs, in 1868; and from this time until his death in 1886, at one of those Bayreuth festivals which but for him could not have existed, we see him in a sort of apotheosis, making a triumphal progress each year from Rome to Weimar and from Weimar to Pesth, the beloved teacher, the admired composer, the revered abbé, the distinguished gentleman. Phase five, in which he is named simply "The Master," is thus a sort of composite and bright blending of all the other incarnations. Hear the description, by an eye-witness, of his appearance at this time:[1] "He is the most interesting and striking man imaginable, tall and slight, with deep-set eyes, shaggy eyebrows, and iron-gray hair. He wears a long abbé's coat, reaching nearly to his feet. His mouth turns up at the corners, which gives, when he smiles, a most crafty and Mephistophelean expression. His hands are very narrow, with long, slender fingers, which look as if they had twice as many joints as other people's. They are so flexible and supple

[1] Amy Fay, "Music Study in Germany."

that it makes you nervous to look at them. Anything like the polish of his manners I never saw. When he got up to leave his box, for instance, after his adieus to the ladies, he laid his hand on his heart and made his final bow, with a quiet courtliness which made you feel that no other way of bowing to a lady was right or proper. His variety of expression is wonderful. One moment his face will look dreamy, shadowy, tragic, the next insinuating, amiable, ironic, sarcastic. All Weimar adores him. When he goes out, every one greets him as if he were a king."

"All Weimar adores him," — let us confess, for we can no longer blink the fact, that there is something nauseous about the atmosphere in which Liszt lived, and that we cannot acquit him of a liking for it. Does not every man choose, at least within certain limitations set by fate, his own environment? Was Liszt entirely indifferent to the attentions of the Polish countess who received him in a boudoir spread ankle-deep with rose leaves, or of the four celebrated beauties who had their portraits painted as Caryatides supporting his bust ? [1]   Was it the sleep of boredom, or of comfortable self-satisfaction, that swathed him on that occasion when he was "discovered sitting on a high platform surrounded by all sorts of pianos and harmoniums, and in full view of six or eight ladies, several of whom were busy fixing his striking features on canvas ?" [2]   Was it pure kindness to a young literary woman that prompted him to invite Janka Wohl to his house to partake of "*un répas tres appétissant,*" and to read aloud to him afterwards "*l'article biographique sur F. L. que nons avons commencé hier*" ? If this same Janka Wohl, who by the way was one of those flattering friends from whom the proverb prays Heaven to preserve us, had said to Beethoven, or Schumann, or Brahms what she said to Liszt: "The others play pieces beautifully, but you always play the soul, the thoughts, and the sentiments of Liszt. You transport us into a world which will die with you, and of which we shall have nothing left but the paradise of recollection — a

[1] Janka Wohl, "Recollections of Liszt," Eng. trans., p. 9.

[2] *Ibid.*, p. 187.

paradise out of which, as the poets say, we cannot be driven" — would these great self-forgetful artists have given her such an answer as Liszt's: "Come, come, it is you who are the poet, dear child; but perhaps there is some truth in what you say"? No, if the idealist in Liszt was often smothered and drugged into lethargy by this miasma of flattery, it was still within his power to seek a clearer, more inspiring air. And it was because he did not do so that there grew up beside the idealist in him that other ego of the poseur and charlatan; and it is his fault as well as his misfortune that posterity will see him, as a youth, posturing in Schaffer's studio, and, as an old man, laying his hand on the left lapel of his abbé's coat as he bows to the ladies in his box.

These grimaces and airs, thin masks as they are to the heart of the man, have unfortunately projected themselves over into his music, and what is more surprising, have imposed upon countless listeners, and even trained critics, who have somehow failed to discern their artificiality. They are traceable chiefly in the fundamental themes; for however skilfully a musician may master his technic, however much he may learn to make of his original ideas by a clever treatment, he cannot materially alter these ideas themselves, which are, so to speak, the instinctive thoughts of his mind; in them he stands revealed for what he finally and essentially is. Now, despite all the mental virtuosity with which Liszt develops his ideas, a virtuosity as astounding, and possibly as deceptive, as the physical virtuosity for which he is more famous, the ideas themselves are for the most part commonplace. They are not spontaneous expressions of his own feeling, but studied efforts to impress his audience. They strut and maunder before us just as "The Master" strutted and maundered, tossed his hair, fixed his eyes on heaven, threw his hands in air, crouched over the keys, smiled and almost wept, before his audience. They are written, not from the heart, but "to the gallery"; their magniloquence is rhetoric, their sparkle is of tinsel, their sentiment is sentimentality. Liszt does not alternate, like Beethoven, Schumann, Tschaïkowsky, or any composer who is profoundly in earnest, between manly force and feminine tenderness;

he alternates between empty pomposity and equally empty mawkishness.

In these thematic counterfeits of his he makes remarkably plausible imitations of the real thing. Take, for example, the first theme of his piano sonata in B-minor (Figure XXVIII),

Figure XXVIII.

a grandiloquent recitative in octaves. This sounds magnificent enough at a first hearing, with its strongly individualized rhythm, its staccato notes followed by pauses, its exciting use of the diminished seventh harmonies; but on longer acquaintance its theatricality, its obvious artificiality, its purely rhetorical effectiveness, become only too apparent; like a sentence printed all in italics, it is impotent through very excess of emphasis. Or take the well-known opening motive of the E-flat Piano Concerto. With its attention-seizing rhythm and its chro-

matic melody it seems at first fraught with un-
told meaning, a fiat, an edict, a proclamation.
But what does it proclaim ? Little, it turns out
as we go on, except that the composer intends
to electrify his hearer; and the hearer, at first
duly astonished, gradually becomes indifferent.
"Give him a piece of bread," said Wagner of
Liszt, "he will cover it with red pepper." So
with the main themes of the "Faust" and
"Dante" symphonies. He is too anxious to
impress us with the vague emotions, the indefinable thrills, of his chromatic harmonies.
Both themes are so insistently chromatic that
the listener's mind becomes satiated, jaded,
numbed. Wagner knew how to manage these
things better when, in his "Pilgrim's March,"
he relieved the wonderful chromatic passage
beginning at the seventeenth measure by setting
against it the simple, strong triad harmonies of
the opening.

If Liszt is unrestrained in his use of the italics
and points of exclamation of the musical language, so that his impressiveness generally
degenerates into ranting, when he tries the
emotional he fairly wallows. It is hard to find

a parallel in any other composer for those
passages of his, fairly redolent with sentimentality, in which he reiterates, over and over
again, a single note, as the poet rolls under his
tongue his mistress's name, or the gourmand,
under his, a morsel of *paté de fois gras*. (See
Figure XXIX, *a* and *b*.) It is hard, in any

Figure XXIX.
(*a*) From the Piano Sonata in B-minor.

(*b*) From the Liebestraum No. 3.
Poco allegro, con affetto.

dolce cantando.

etc.

other composer who has had the advantage of German traditions, to find bits of melody so feebly Italian, so sunk in an amiable but insidious sensuality, as the themes of his "Son-

netto del Petrarca" or his Album Leaf no. 2,
in which he writes with the pen dipped in
violet water of a Donizetti or a Bellini. His
harmonic idiom, too, is degraded by a similar
sensuality, however disguised. How else than
as proceeding from a love for thrills and swoons
can we explain his passion for those chords,
such as diminished sevenths, minor ninths, and
all manner of chromatically altered chords, as
the theorists call them, which, for some reason
never yet explained, exhale mawkishness as
some women exhale musk ? [1]

It would be interesting, did it not involve a
general discussion here out of place, to inquire
how far the exaggerated expression of Liszt is
due to the lack of spiritual, moral, and intellectual balance already noted as characteristic
of French romanticism. Surely there is more
than a striking analogy, there is an actual
relation of cause and effect, were we but learned

---

[1] See, as examples of this cloying harmonization, both
excerpts in Figure XXIX, or almost any of the "Consola-
tions" and "Liebesträume." An especially flagrant
instance may be found in the Piano Sonata in B-minor,
edition of Breitkopf and Härtel, p. 29, the last measure.

and keen enough to trace it out, between the unrestrained individualism of the romanticist, in politics, religion, love — and the hysterical, unreal feeling of this music.   Both alike lose poise by taking an over-personal view of life.   Liszt, so singly set on being magnificent or heart-rending in passion that he ignores the restraints of good taste, forgets artistic reserve, and becomes in turn blustering and craven, reminds us of Rousseau, so in love with his fixed idea of "freedom" that he undermines the foundations of the social order on which true freedom depends.

If Liszt were quite sincere in his passionate extremes, we should have to forgive them as on the whole we forgive the often crude grandiloquence of the Gallic Berlioz.   What makes the Hungarian artist peculiarly exasperating is the impression of hypocrisy in his heroics that we cannot escape or argue away.   He does not really feel these things, we discern; he is ogling us, he is posing for our benefit; all the while that one of his eyes is so proudly flashing fire, or so devoutly gazing heavenward, or so touchingly secreting a tear, the other is winking

at his *alter ego*, the ego that sits behind the
scenes and pulls the strings. What those ladies
to whom he bowed with such an irresistible
chivalry, such a noble humility, would have
felt could they have read the cynical thoughts
about women which meanwhile filled his mind,
that we feel when we realize that for all his
pompous utterance, for all his dreamy emotion,
he is in his heart laughing at us for being so
obligingly impressed by his rhodomontade. We
can forgive, we can even rather enjoy, the poseur
who is himself in love with his pose, but not the
charlatan who makes capital of our gullibility.

Liszt shows to far better advantage, however, in his manipulation of his ideas than in
the ideas themselves; for whereas in the latter
artificiality is a damning fault, in the former
art, especially such skilful art as his, is a shining
merit. His plan of combining the musical
organization of the classicists with the dramatic
organization of Berlioz was an interesting and
in some ways a felicitous one. By the use of
program and leading motives he secured the
advantages of the realistic school: freedom
from the shackles of the strict traditional

sonata-form, and a "poetic" principle of coherence. By retaining thematic development, he reënforced this poetic coherence by musical logic, and avoided to some extent the fragmentary effects into which unmodified realism generally falls. To the ~~thirteen~~ orchestral pieces in which he most strikingly embodied this plan of interlinked dramatic and musical structure he gave the name of "Poëmes Symphoniques," generally translated as "Symphonic Poems" though more precisely as "Orchestral Poems." He owes his chief historical importance to his creation of this form, which he exemplified also on a larger scale in his "Faust" and "Dante" symphonies.

A brief analysis of his most popular symphonic poem, "Les Préludes," will make clear the peculiarities of the type. This work has a program, taken from Lamartine's "Méditations poetiques," as follows: —

"What is our life but a series of Preludes to that unknown song of which death strikes the first solemn note? Love is the enchanted dawn of every life; but where is the destiny in which the first pleasures of happiness are not interrupted by some storm, whose deadly breath dissipates its fair illusions, whose fatal thunderbolt consumes its altar ?   And where is the soul which, cruelly wounded, does not seek, at the coming of one of these storms, to calm its memories in the tranquil life of the country ? Man, however, cannot long resign himself to the kindly tedium which has at first charmed him in the companionship of nature, and when 'the trumpet has sounded the signal of alarms,' he hastens to the post of peril, whatever may be the strife which calls him to its ranks, in order to regain in combat the full consciousness of himself and the complete command of his powers."

This program, it will at once be seen, is far more favorable to musical treatment than Berlioz's hotch-potches of petty details and wild, incongruous fancies.   It is but slightly narrative and descriptive, presenting rather such abstract emotional states as music can best depict.   And it has a natural symmetry and completeness of its own which the composer has only to reproduce in order to give his music the same desirable qualities.   This he does by dividing his piece into six sections, which might be called

Introduction, Love, Storm, Country Life, War, and Coda or Conclusion.

To this natural poetic structure Liszt adds a most ingenious musical form, by basing his entire work on two leading motives (*a* and *b* in Figure XXX), which he subjects to all

Figure XXX.

manner of variation, melodic, harmonic, rhythmic, as opportunity suggests. Some of the more important of these variants, set down in Figures XXX–XXXIII, deserve careful attention. The work begins with a recitative for strings, andante (*c*), derived from (*a*) by a modification of rhythm. At page 7 of the full orchestral score, published by Breitkopf and Härtel, appears another variant of the same theme, andante maestoso in bass strings and brass (*d*). Motive (*a*) is sung by the 'cellos, in very nearly its primitive form, at page 13 (*e*); in the last measure of this excerpt the very clever echoing of the three characteristic notes of the theme, in the bass, marked by asterisks, should be especially noted. Motive (*b*), symbolizing love, first appears at page 21, sensuously set forth by four horns, strings, and harp, is taken up by the wood wind, and is developed in a powerful climax, at the end of which appears for a moment the variant of it represented at (*f*). Thus in the first two sections of the poem are the underlying motives expounded and somewhat developed.

Section three, Storm, begins (allegro ma non

troppo, page 30) with a very theatrical variant of motive *a*, highly characteristic of Liszt, in which he resorts to the chromatic scale beloved of all musical storm-makers (*g*, Figure XXXI),

Figure XXXI.
(*g.*)

(*h.*)

and later to an endless series of diminished sevenths, intended for nothing but to make our flesh creep (*h*). It is unnecessary to follow out this section in detail; it is the least interesting of all, and illustrates that element of claptrap which Liszt could never entirely eliminate.

The mood now changes again, and with (*i*) (Figure XXXII), a charmingly expanded version

Figure XXXII.
(*i.*)

(*j.*)

of motive *a*, intrusted to the oboe, an allegretto pastorale is ushered in, beginning the fourth section, Country Life. A new theme, of fascinating grace and freshness (*j*), now enters in the horn, and is presently combined with motive *b* in what seems on the whole the most delightful moment, musically, of the entire composition (*k*). A somewhat lengthy working out of these combined motives follows, gradually growing more and more agitated, until, with an adaptation of the protean motive (*a*) for horns and trumpets, allegro marziale (*l*) (Figure XXXIII), the fifth section, War, is introduced. Piccolos and drums become prominent, and at page 82 of the score even the love motive (*b*) takes on a militant character (*m*, Figure XXXIII). Turmoil now increases steadily until a sort of apotheosis is reached with the reëntrance of the majestic passage (*d*), in Figure XXX, and the poem comes to an impressive close.

Figure XXXIII.

The advantages of such a scheme of form as is exemplified in "Les Préludes" are many; and they are made the most of by Liszt, with his accustomed cleverness and long-headed sense for practical values. For both of the two classes of listeners that make up the average concert audience music made on this recipe has an appropriate appeal. That class, usually a majority, which has little ear for music, but likes to indulge itself in vague dreams, pictorial imaginings, and nervous thrills, finds its account in the program, follows out with interest the suggestions of the various moods, such as, in the present instance, the amorous, the stormy, the pastoral, the warlike, and gets its fill, all along the way, of brilliant and gorgeous tone-coloring, exciting rhythms, sombre, rich, or mysterious harmonies. At the same time the minority of true music-lovers have, as they have not in the works of Berlioz, a "logical and lucid play of definite motives" to enjoy; they trace with never failing interest the transformations of a few simple themes; they may entirely forget the program, and yet have plenty of opportunity for an agreeable activity of attention, perception, memory, and imagination. Thus each hearer may pick out from the mass of conglomerate impressions something that appeals to him.

There is a fine freedom about the symphonic poem which degenerates into lawlessness only when the composer's skill is insufficient to hold it firmly in hand. It is not, like the sonata and the symphony, condemned beforehand to follow a certain course, to fill a predetermined mould; it can ramify, as it proceeds, in obedience to its own latent possibilities. A development here may be expanded to great length, an episode or repetition there may be abbreviated to the slightest possible compass; so long as each link securely engages the next, so long as there is no break in the coherence of the thread, the hearer will be satisfied. Through all the twists and turns the presence of the fundamental melodies will save him from that sense of mere drifting which was so painful to Wagner in listening to Berlioz's "Romeo and Juliet." The symphonic poem bears, in fact, somewhat the same relation to the symphony that rhymed couplets bear to a sonnet, triolet, or other conventional verse-form. It exacts little of strict formalism; but by retaining, underneath all its free ramification, certain basic principles of balance and symmetry, it escapes the pitfall of amorphousness, and constantly satisfies, though in unexpected ways, the radical expectations of the intelligent listener.

Unfortunately, however, Liszt himself fell short of realizing the finer potentialities of his own device. Just as his primal melodies, as we have already seen, are usually of a stilted, rhetorical, and artificial character, his treatment of them, the second but scarcely less important of the processes of composition, is generally labored; it is apt to be a clever feat of intelligence, a sort of mental legerdemain, rather

than a spontaneous germination of idea. What
he said of Chopin's larger works, that they
showed "*plus de volunté que d'inspiration,*" is
true of his own. His developments are as often
distortions as fulfilments, and among his melodies there are many monsters. Plausible, and
even winning, as are at first sight some of the
thematic transformations (for we are apt to be
won by any display of intelligence, no matter
how specious its ends), on closer inspection they
are seen to be mere juggling. The variants of
motive (*a*), in "Les Préludes," shown at (*c*)
and (*d*) in Figure XXX, at (*g*) in Figure XXXI,
and at (*l*) in Figure XXXIII, have an unpleasant sub-flavor of artificiality; analysis reveals their derivation from the parent motive,
but affection, so to speak, repudiates them.
Even more is this the case with (*f*) in Figure
XXX, and (*m*) in Figure XXXIII, which,
though we see that they come from motive *b*,
we feel to be parodies or caricatures of it,
bearing only a superficial resemblance to it,
and quite devoid of its essential character.
Such observations make us wonder whether
a theme is not truly as inconvertible into

anything else as any other individual being, and whether the kind of thematic transformation, or deformation, adopted by Liszt, is not after all intrinsically mechanical and inartistic. If the reader will take the trouble to look at some typical example of thematic evolution as it is practised by a master like Beethoven, such as the first movement, for instance, of the "Eroica Symphony,"[1] he will see what a vast difference there is between such inevitable drawing forth of the very soul of a melody, by a process as august and beyond human whim as the processes of nature, and the laborious ingenuity of the composer of "Les Préludes."

As in this all-important matter of thematic development, so is it in other subordinate matters of technic: Liszt, allowing mere ostentation, immediate effect upon an audience, to have too large a part in his artistic ideal, falls thereby into a hundred artificialities. While he was alive the extraordinary magnetism of his personality carried it all off, by disguising the factitiousness of his methods, and reënforc-

[1] See the present author's "Beethoven and his Fore-runners," pp. 316–321.

ing immensely their superficial appeal; but
stripped from himself and scanned in the cold
impersonal light of criticism, his gorgeous
artistic accoutrements look thin and tawdry,
and prove to be made, not of geniune gold, but
of theatrical tinsel. His melody, when it neither
struts nor fawns, is apt to stagnate. His
"furiously chromatic" harmony gains its effectiveness at the expense of solidity; by too completely forgetting key-relationship, on which
all genuine harmony must depend, it falls into
chaos, as the harmony of a master such as
Wagner never does. When it is based on the
old ecclesiastical modes instead of on the chromatic scale, as in many passages of the later
religious works, it is no less a fabrication, an
artifice: the Palestrina-like ending of the
Credo in the "Gran Mass," for example, is
pseudo-mediævalism, such as no modern composer could write spontaneously. His orchestration, much praised, is indeed skilful, but
radically vulgar; his amorous 'cellos and bray-
ing trombones are enemies fatal to artistic
moderation and restraint. Even in his piano-
writing, so large an element in his fame, his

methods are those of barbarism. He ignores the lesson of fitness that Chopin might have taught him, and overstrains the resources of the poor instrument until, instead of achieving its own unique possibilities, it becomes a forlorn imitation of an orchestra, without an orchestra's variety, sonority, and grandeur.

Thus is the virtuoso spirit of Liszt, which had thriven on adulation only too well from the days when, as "*le petit Litz*," he made the tour of the boxes, to those later days when, as "The Master," he oscillated between Rome and Weimar in one prolonged triumph, responsible for errors of taste and judgment which seriously impair the value of all his work. Yet there was in him, besides the virtuoso who fed on applause and was not superior to charlatanisms when they served his purpose, quite another being, who aspired honestly to be a faithful servant of art, and who brought to the service rare intellectual powers. This was the Liszt who befriended all worthy composers, who gave freely of his time, his money, and his strength, whenever he saw merit unacknowledged or genius struggling for bread. This was the

Liszt who kept Wagner alive until the world could learn to appreciate him, who sought out César Franck when he was the obscure organist of St. Clotilde, who risked his post as Kapellmeister in order to produce an opera by his friend Cornelius. And this was the Liszt whose keen wit discerned the principles of combined musical and dramatic form on which works intrinsically far superior to his own were later written by Dvořák, Smetana, Tschaïkowsky, Saint-Saëns, and Richard Strauss. Whatever his purely musical powers, his indefatigable and highly cultivated mind and his generous heart enabled him to play an important rôle in the history of music.